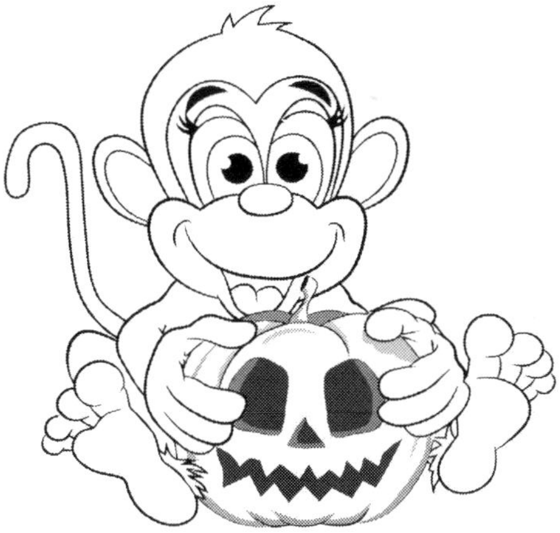

THIS BOOK BELONGS TO

COLOR TEST

TEST YOUR COLOR SUPPLIES ON THIS PAGE TO SEE HOW THEY REACT TO THE PAPER

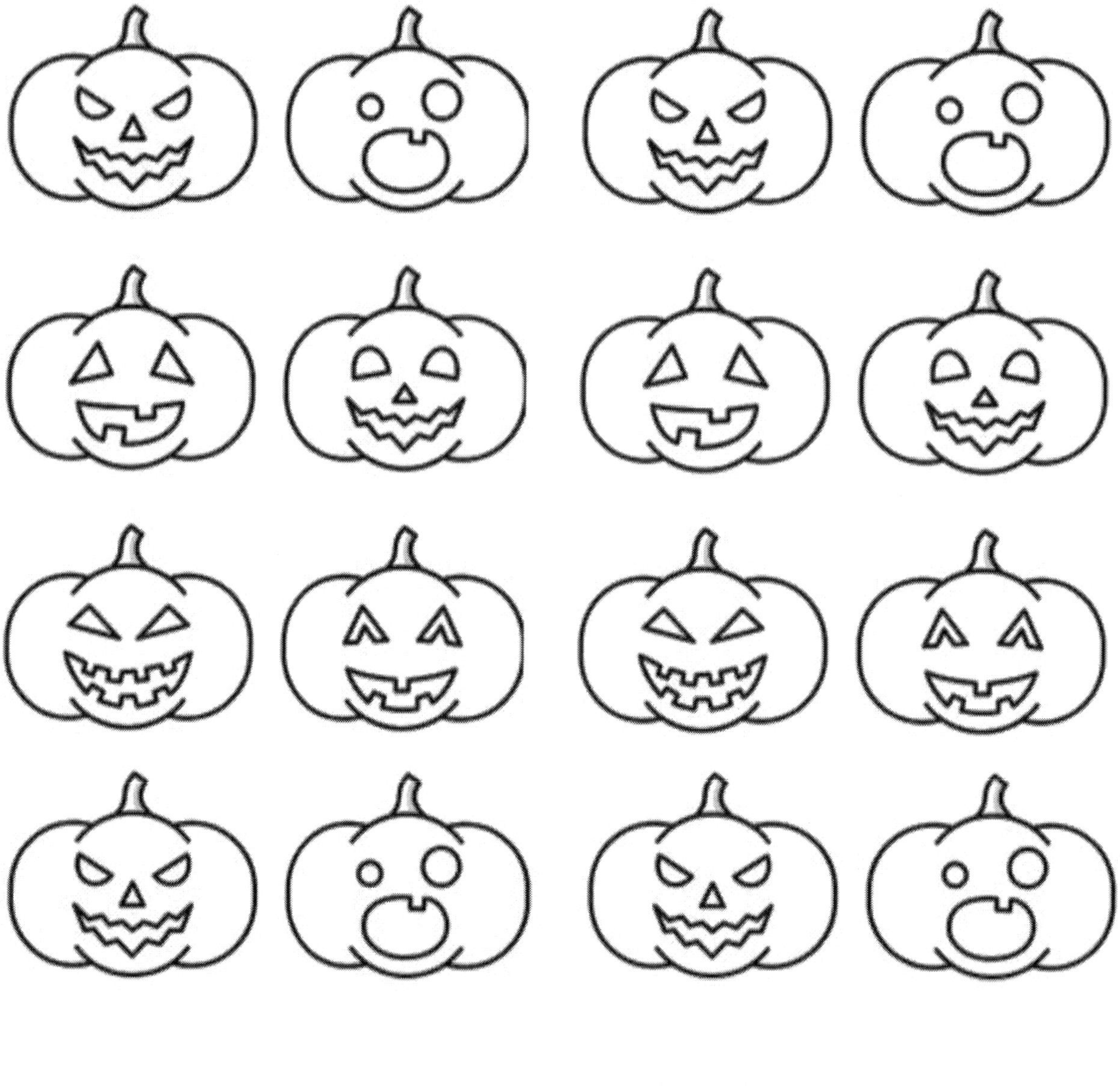

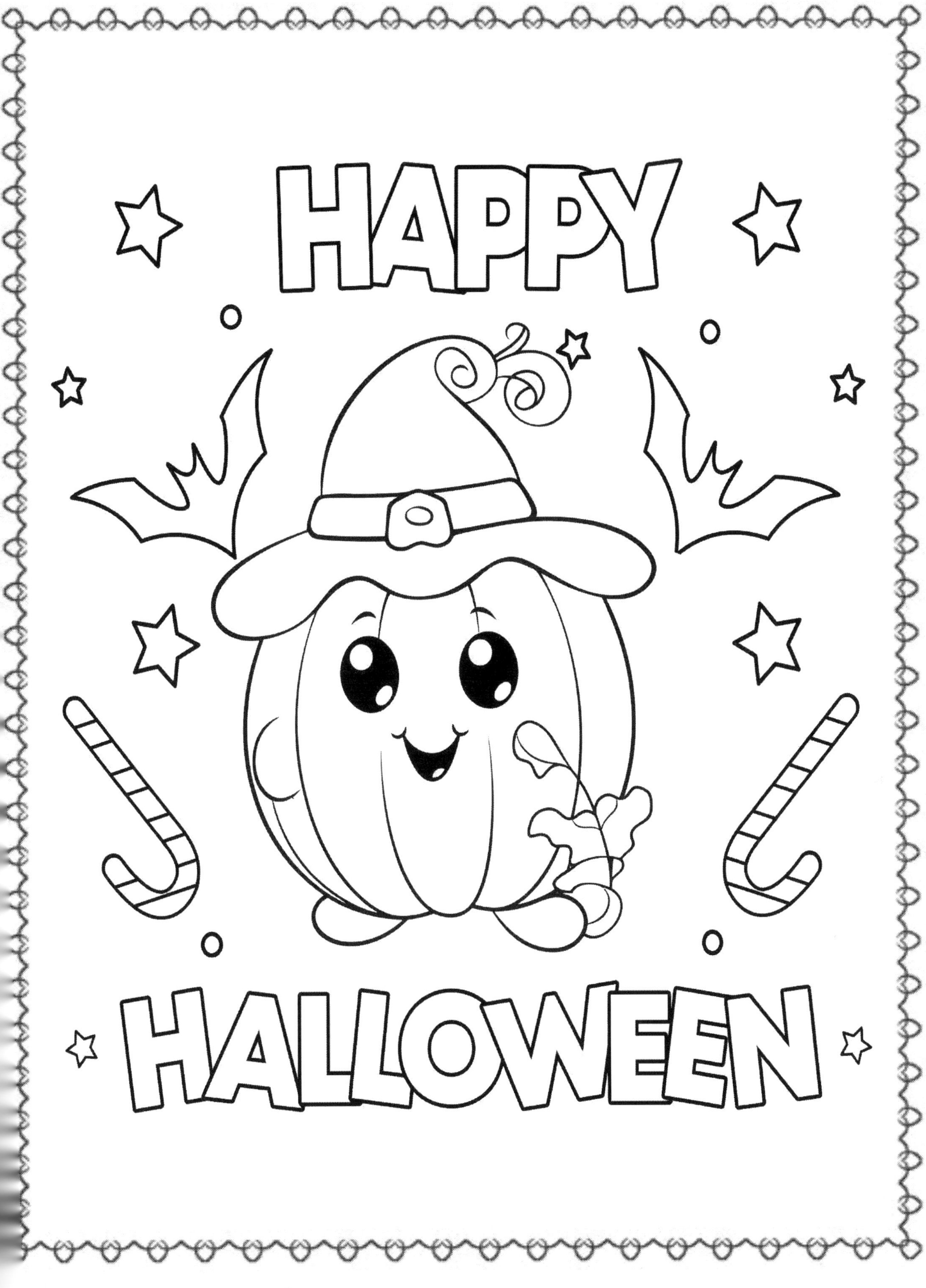
HAPPY
HALLOWEEN

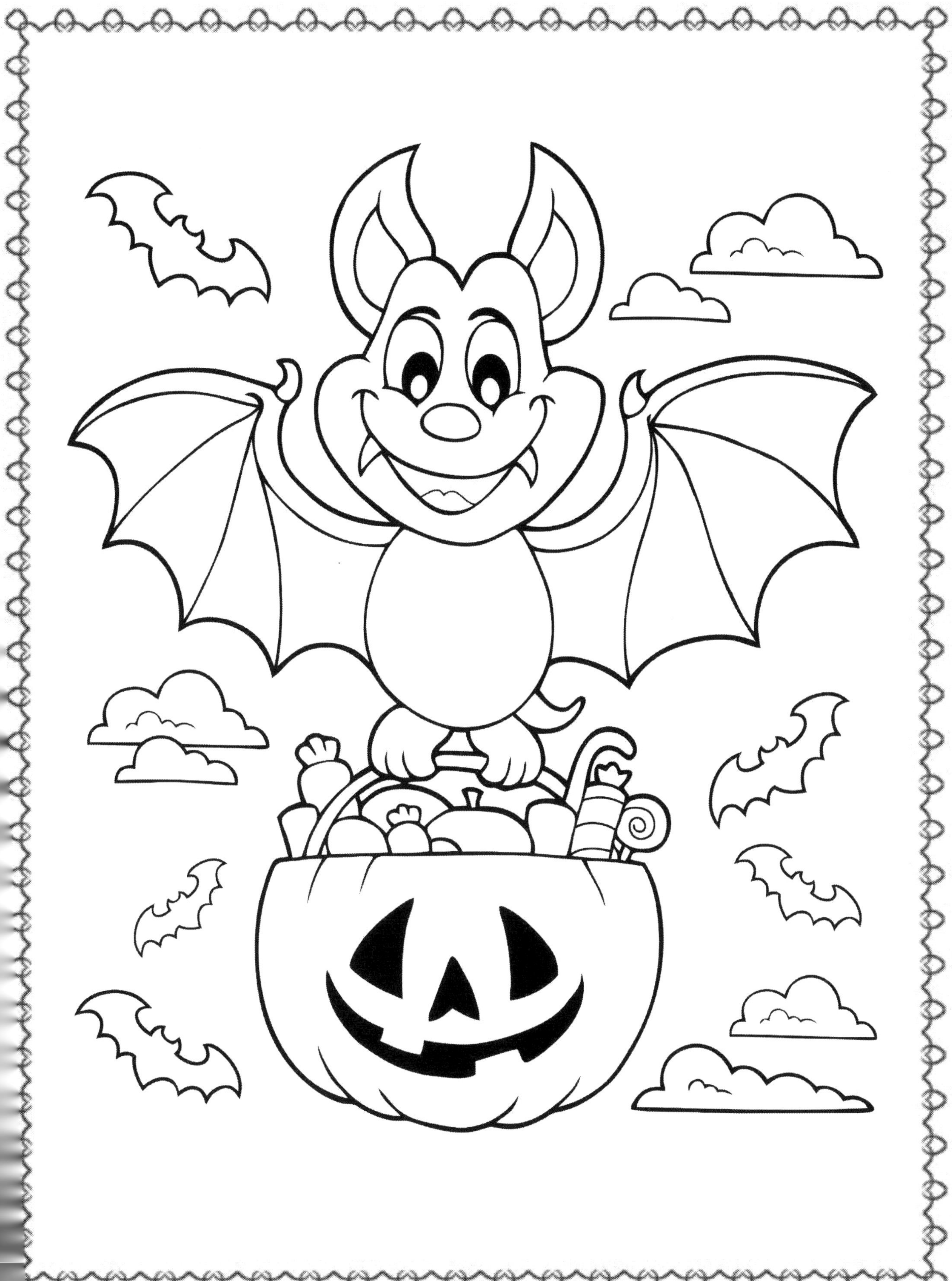

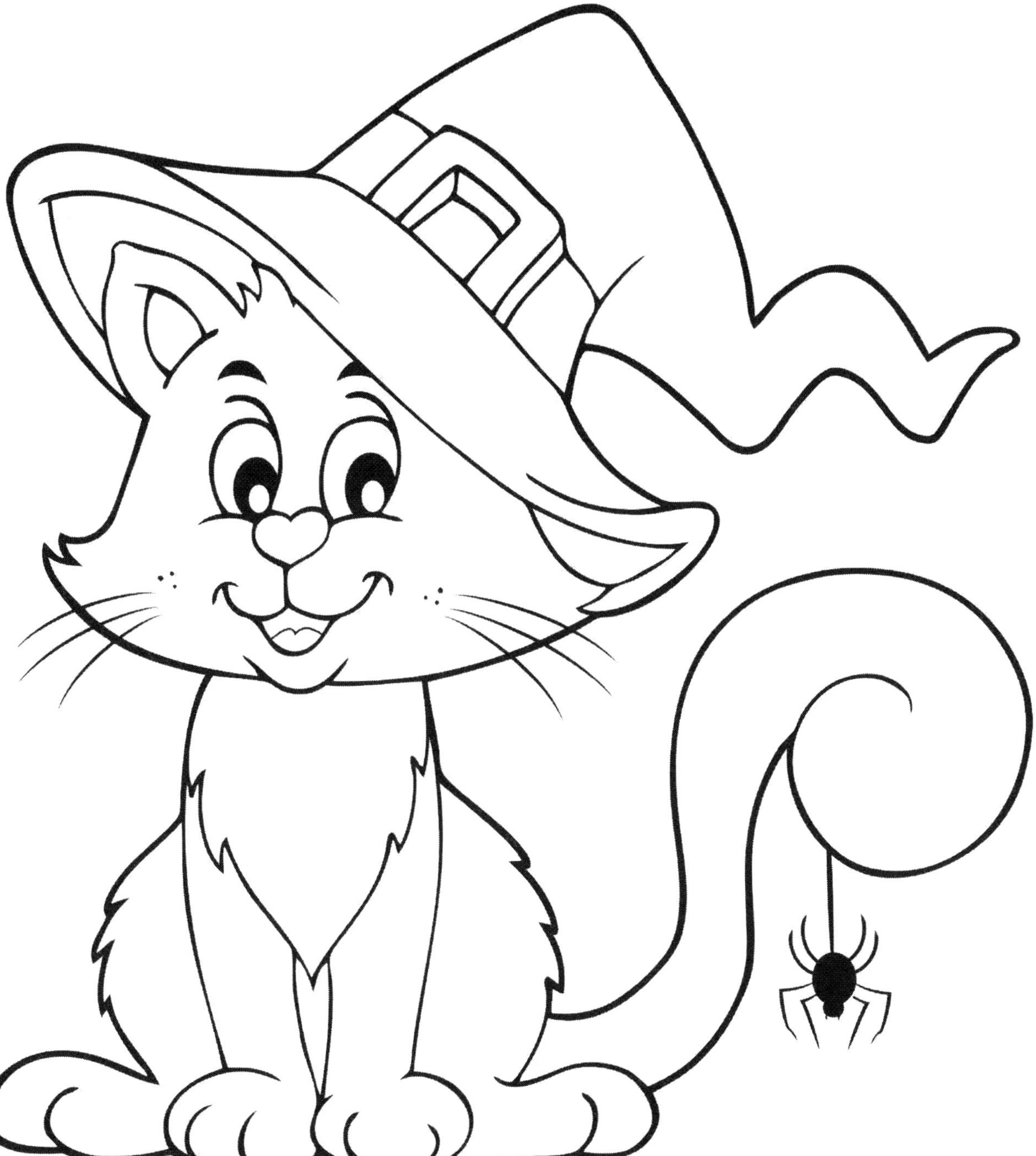

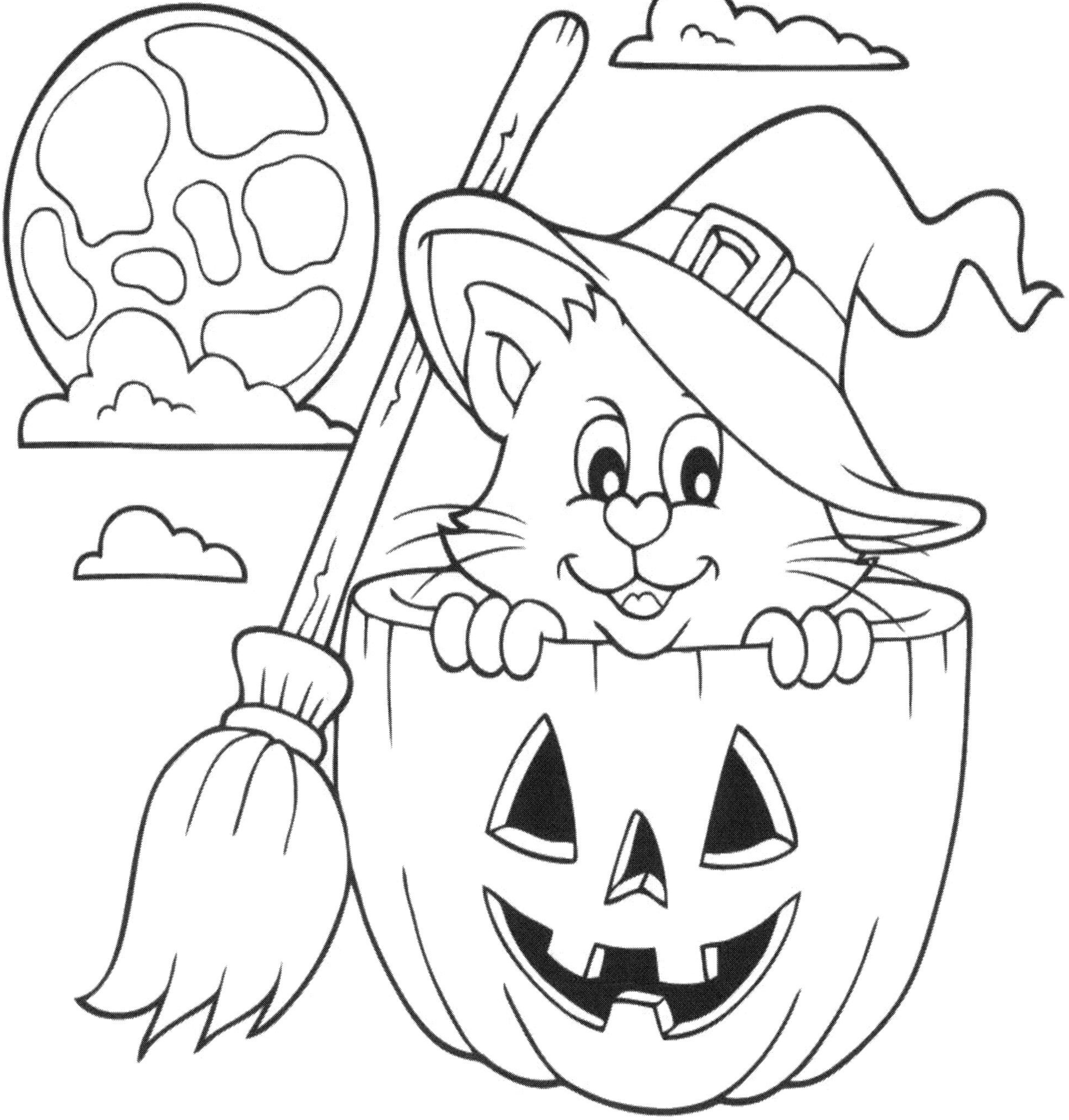

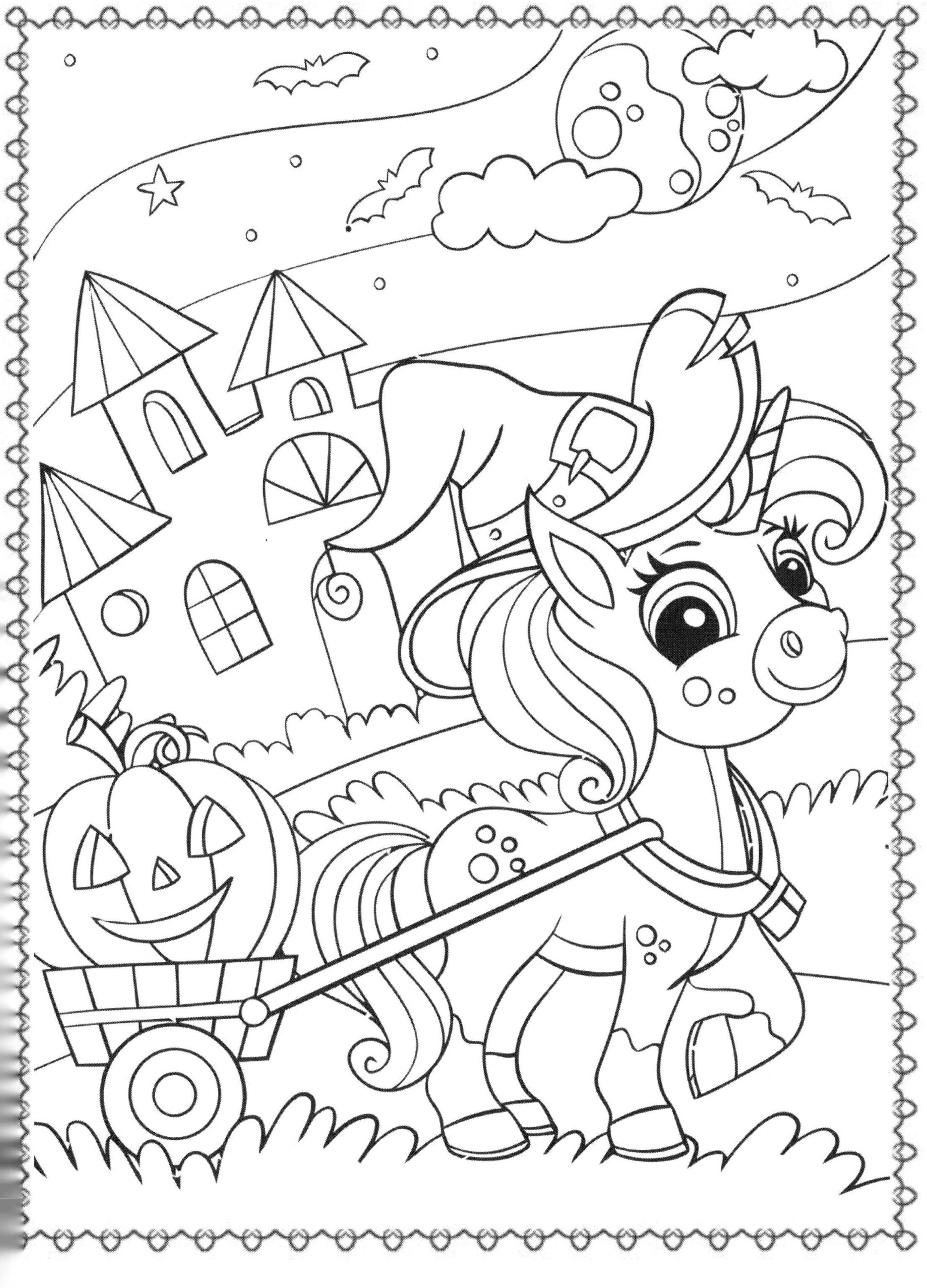

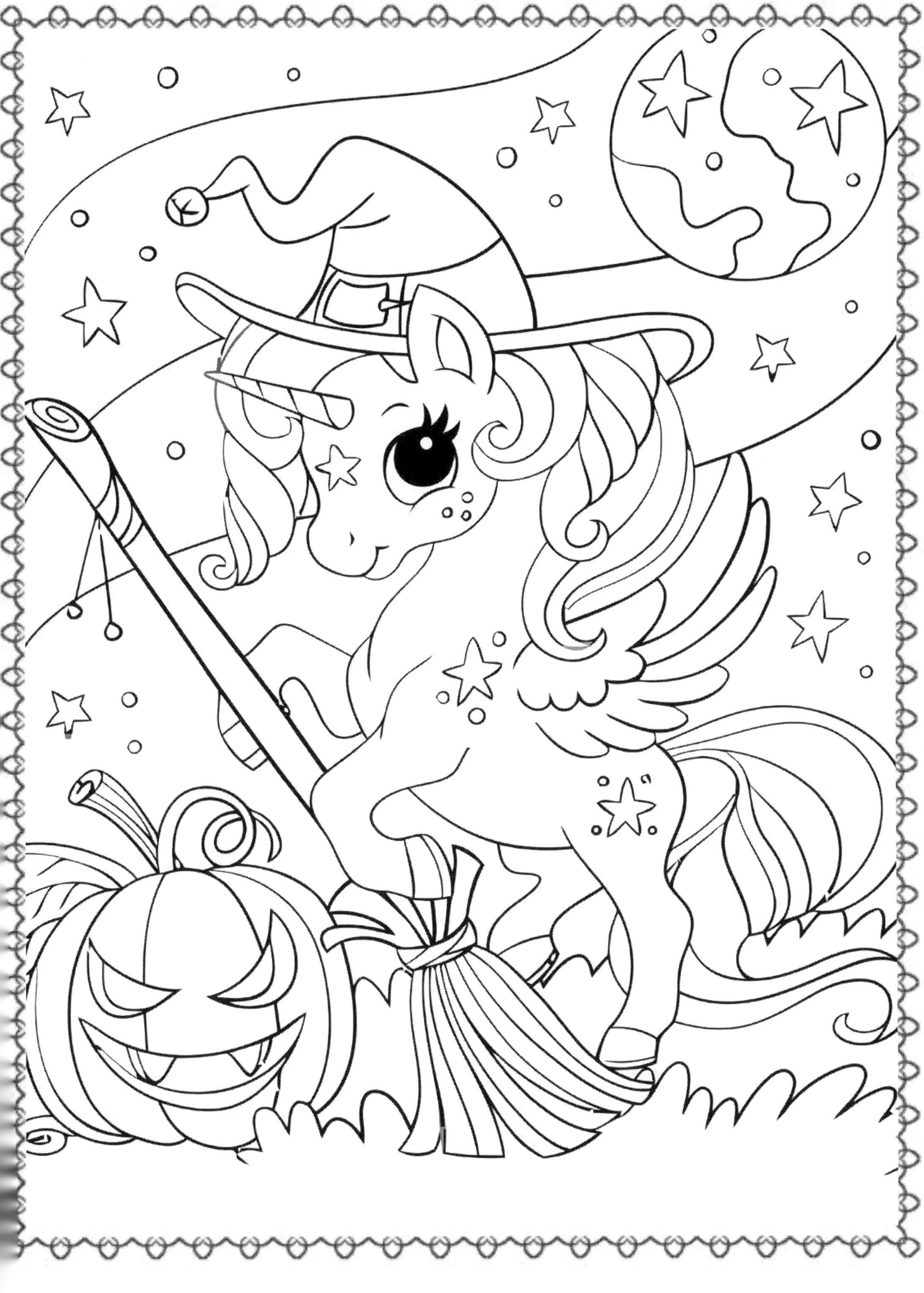

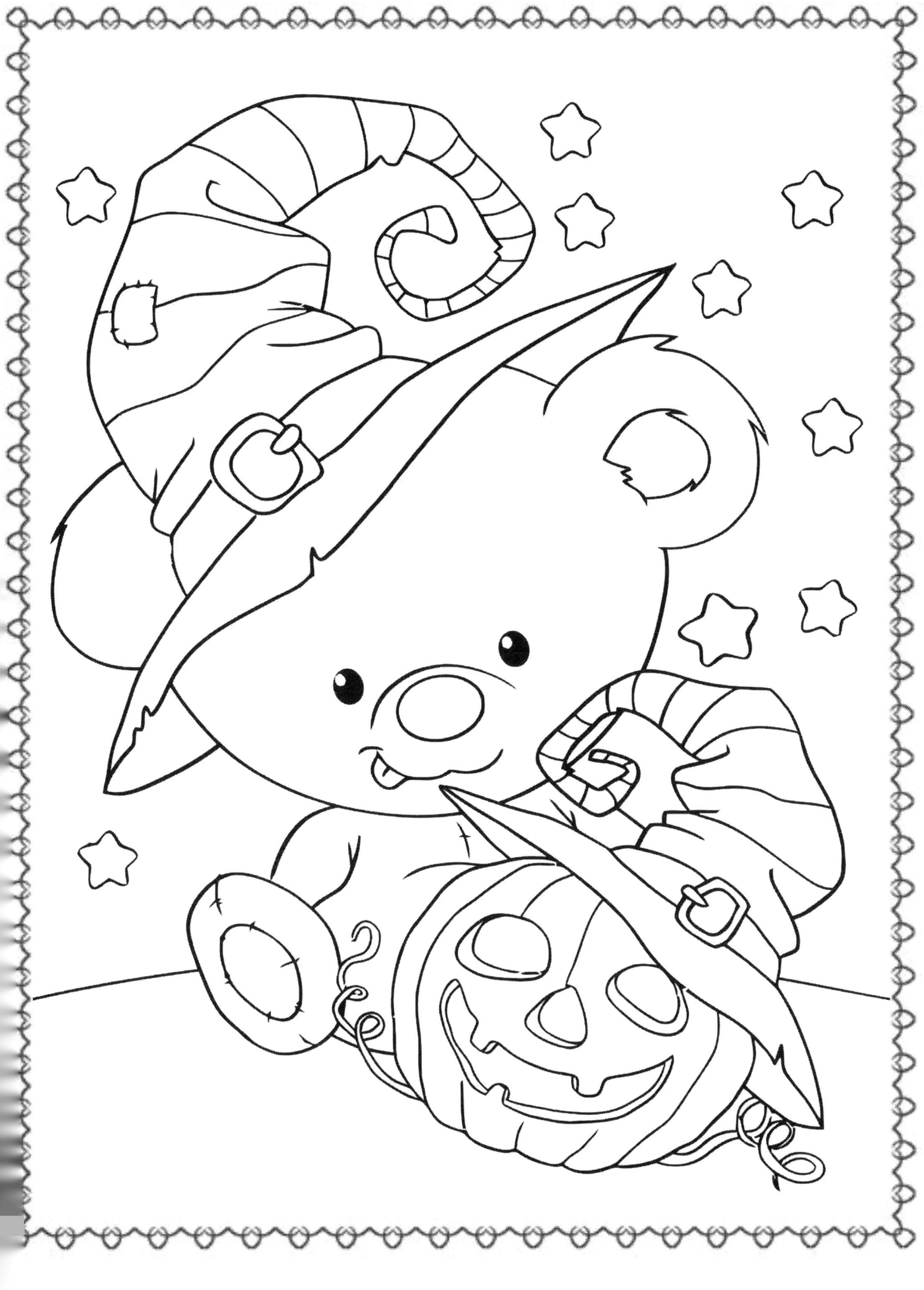

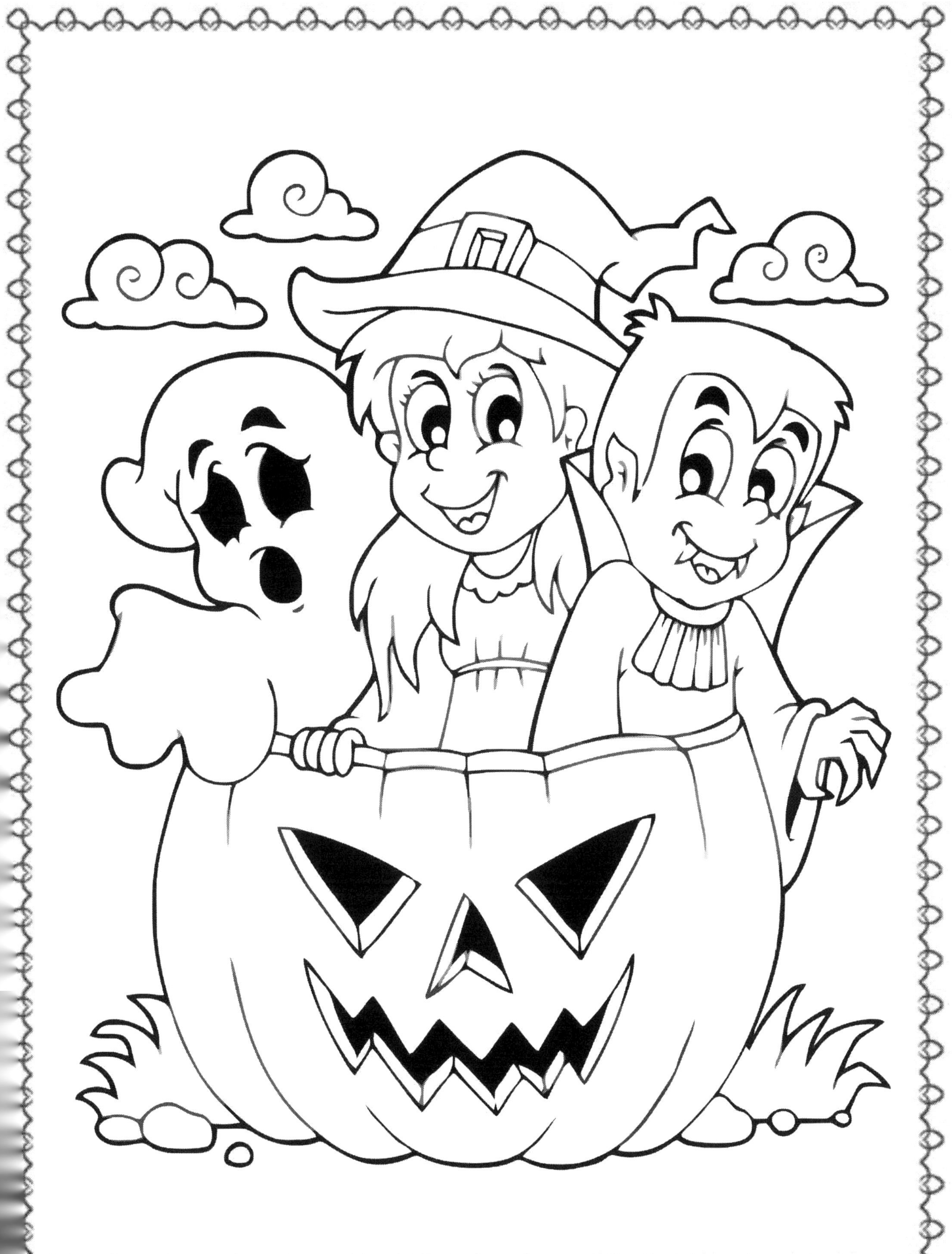

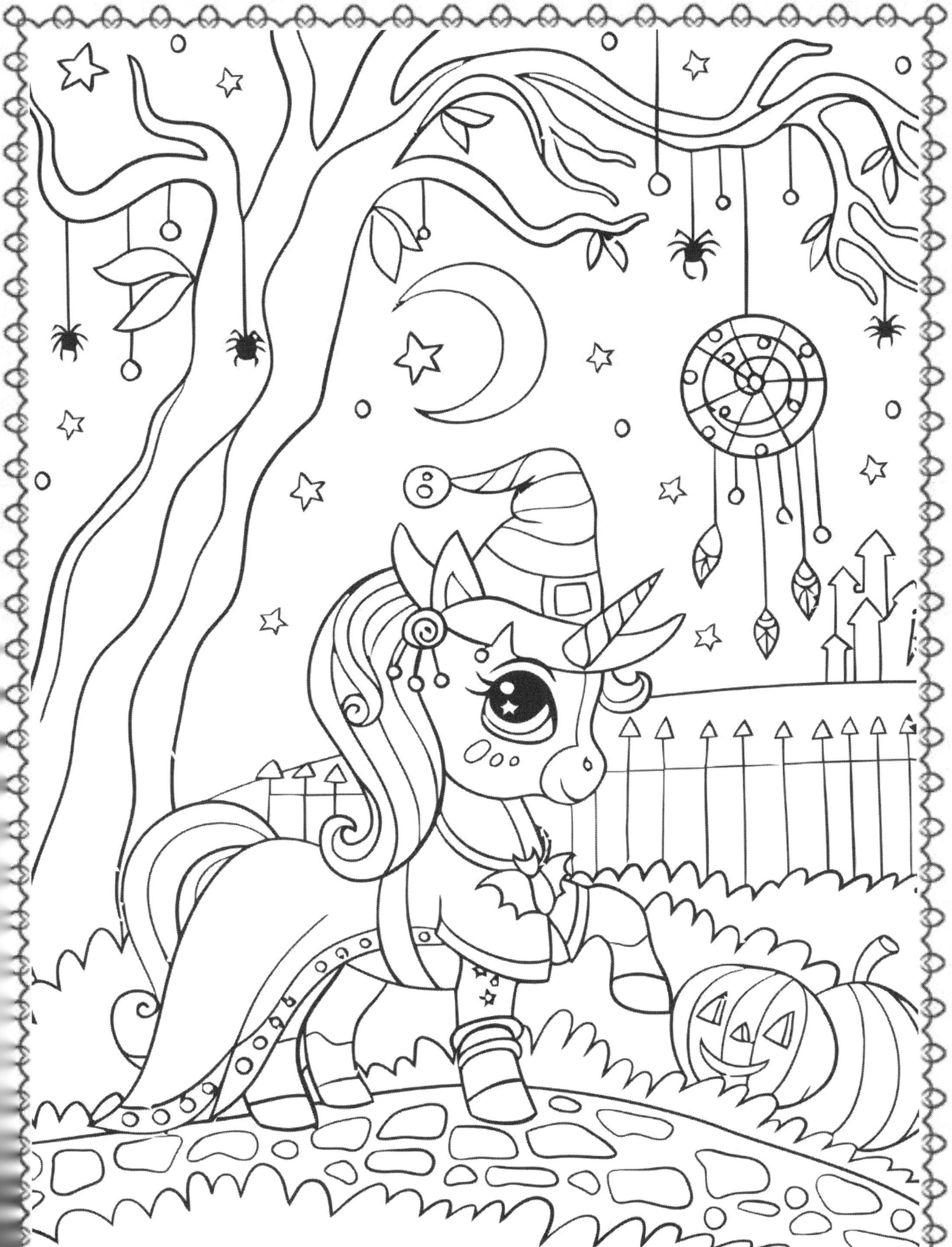

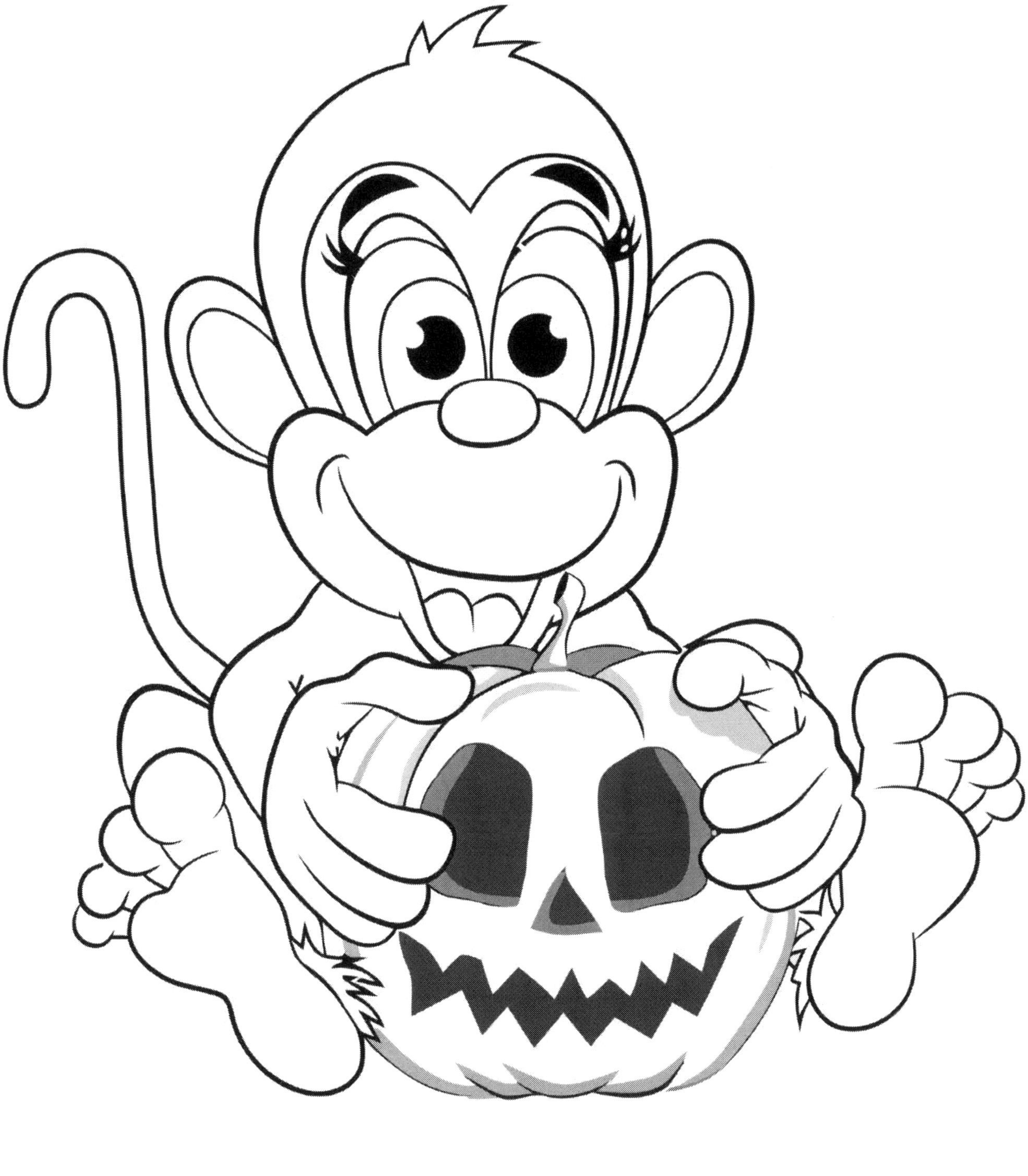

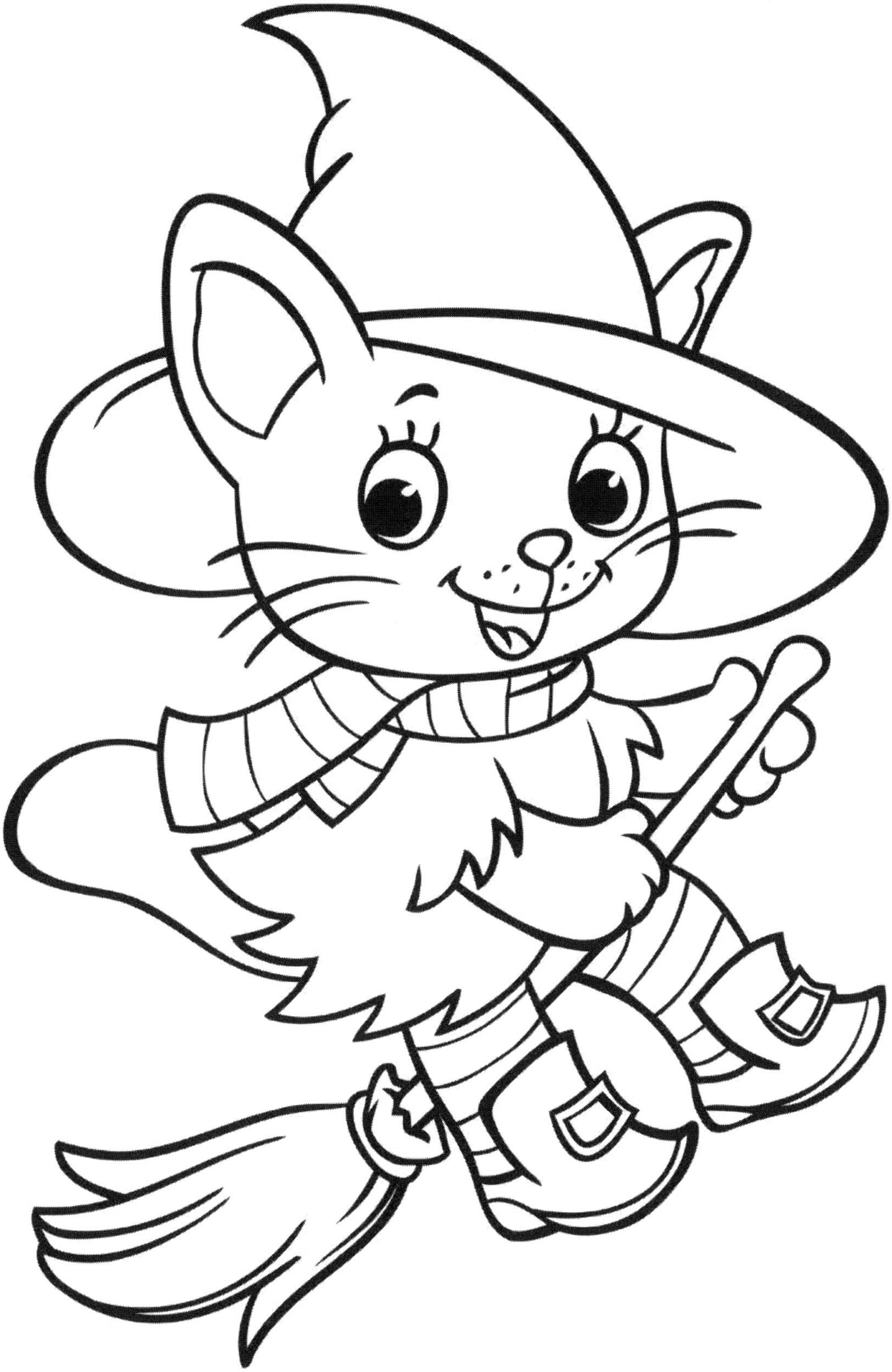

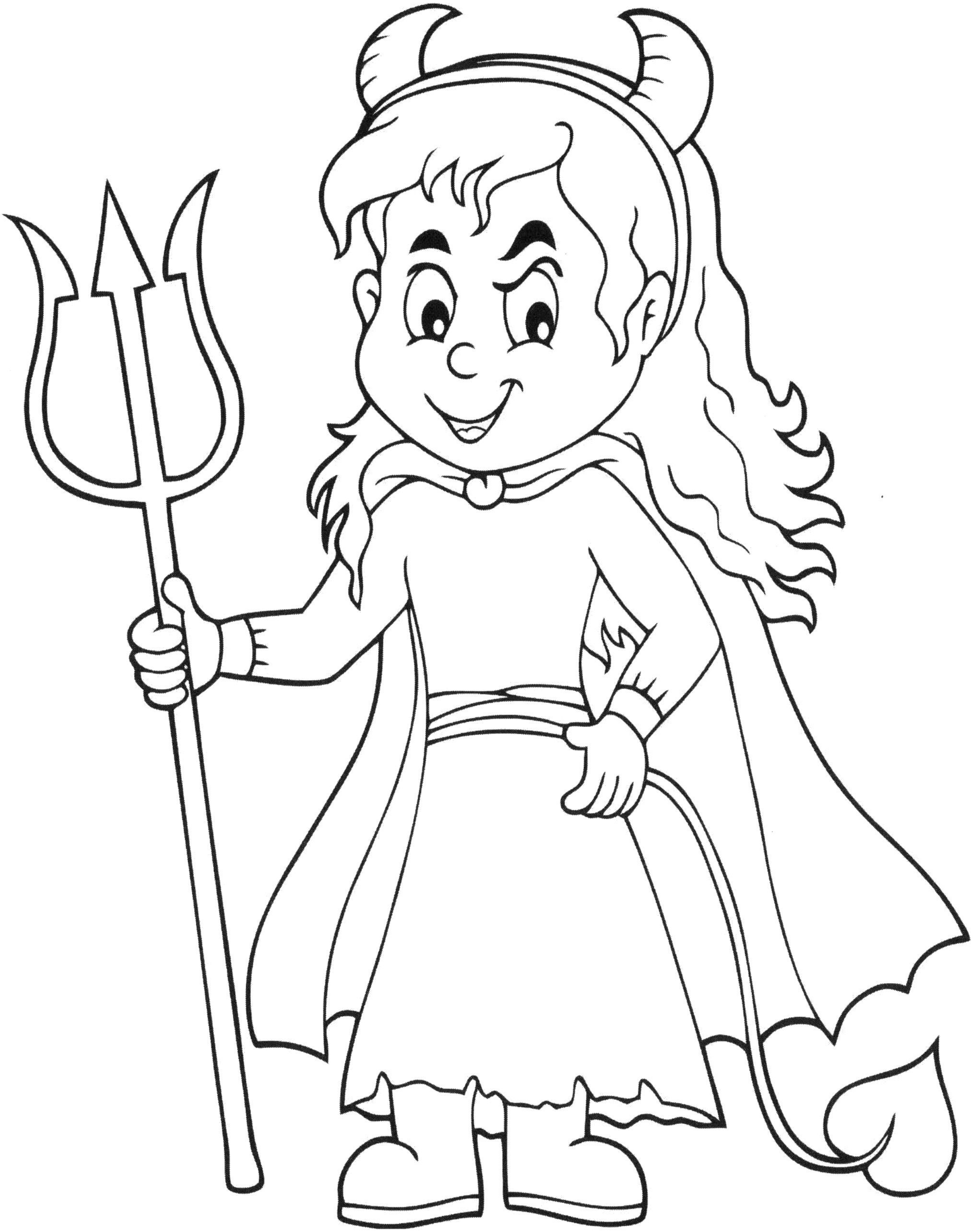

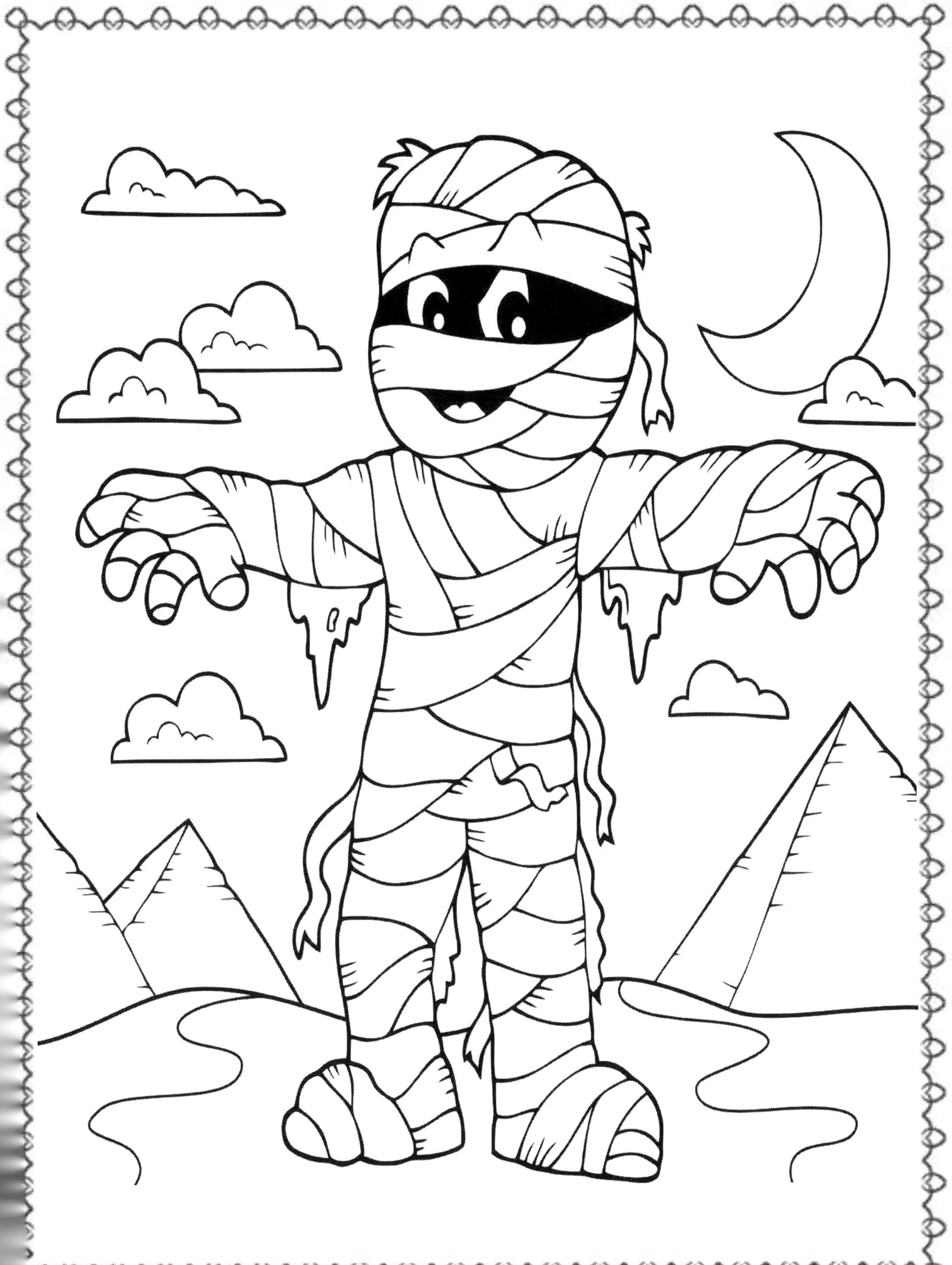

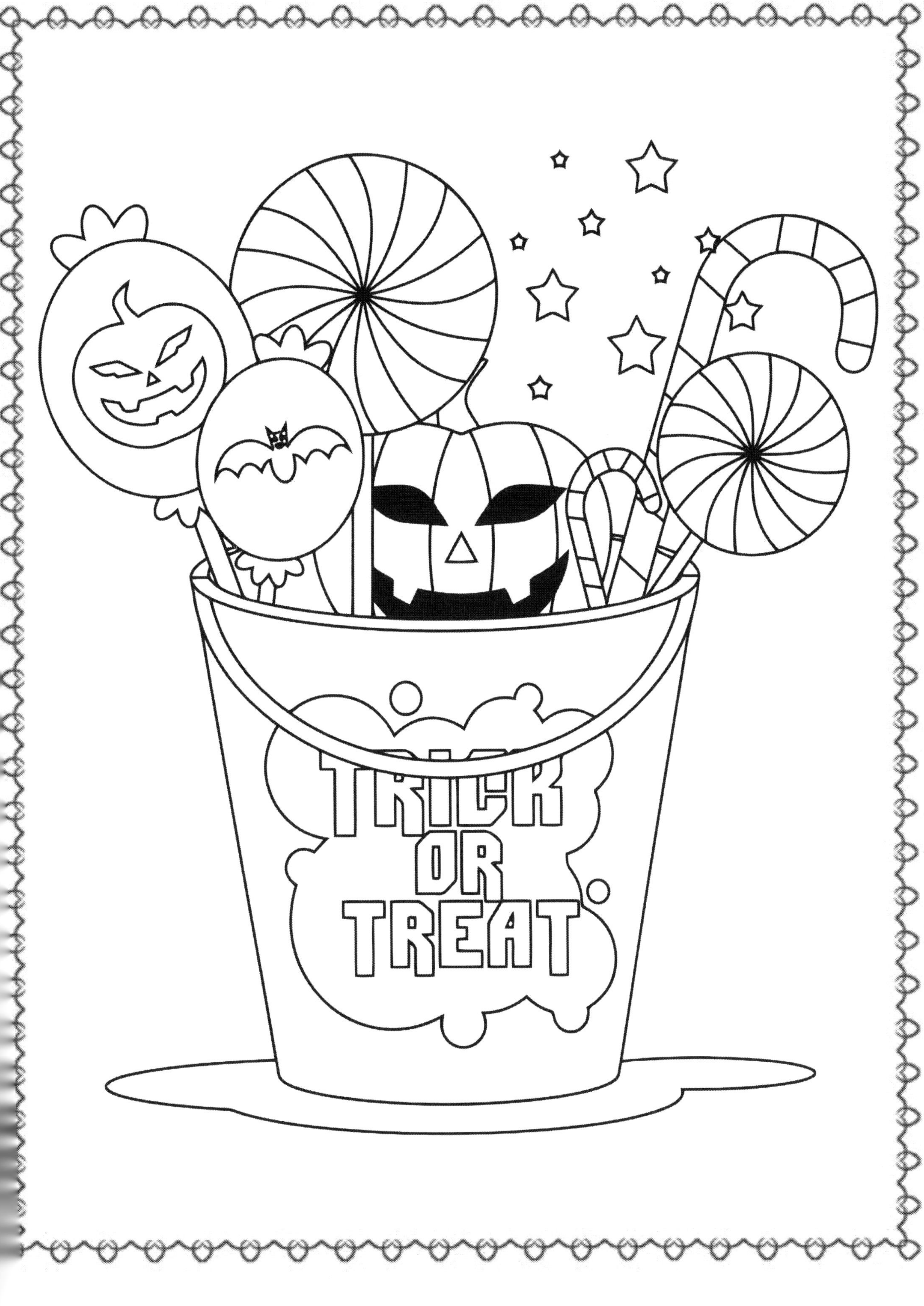
TRICK
OR
TREAT

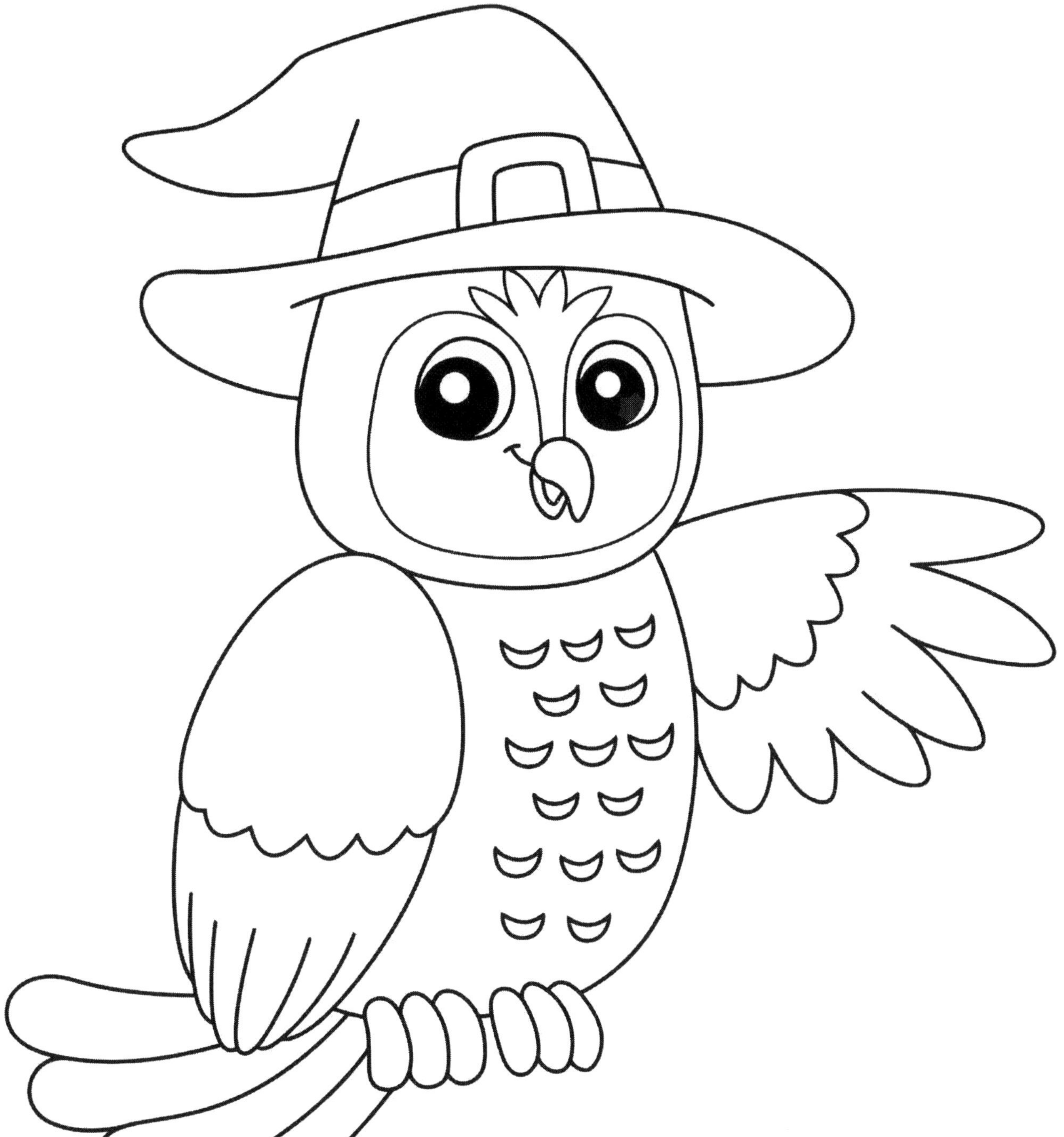

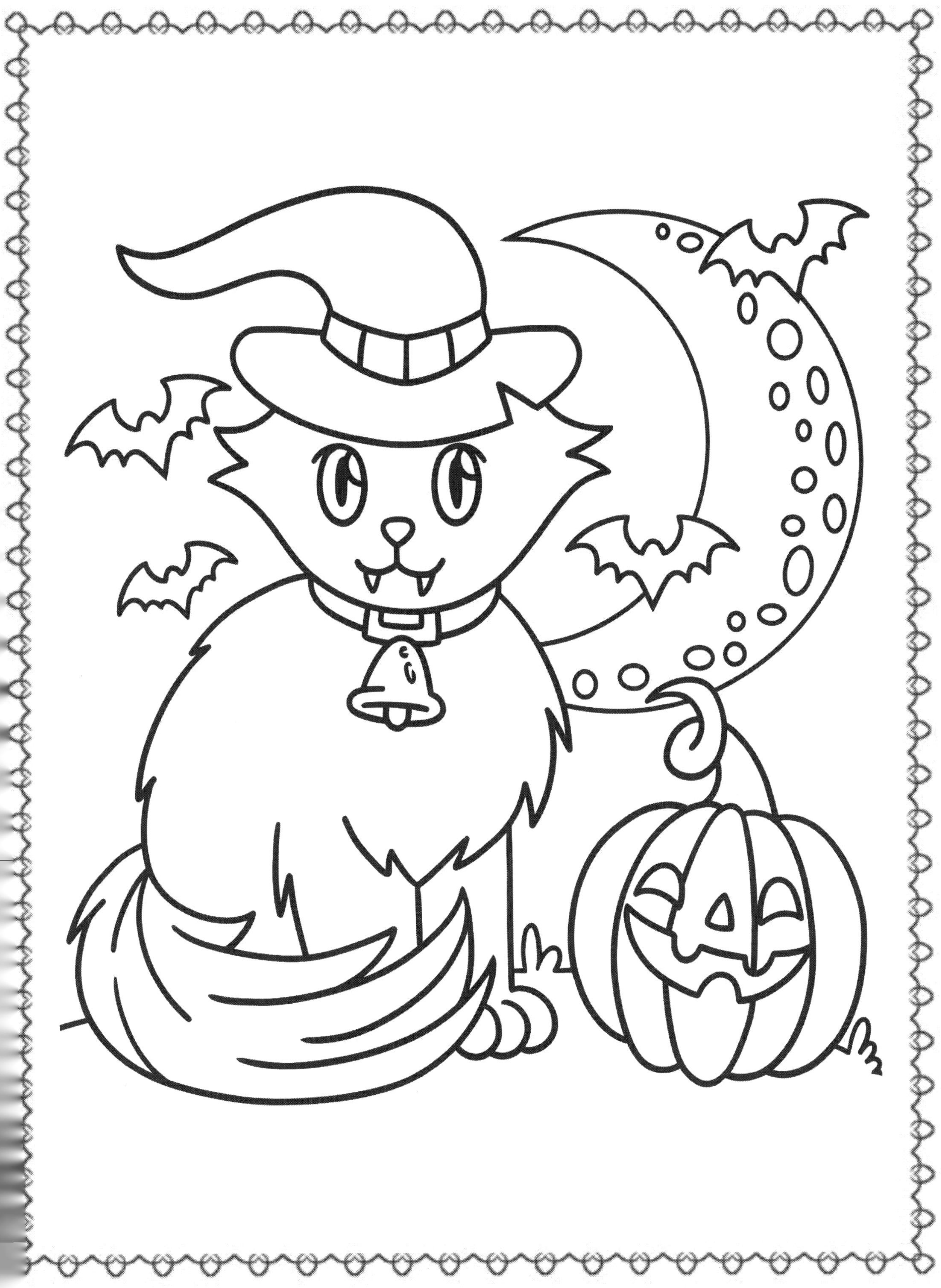

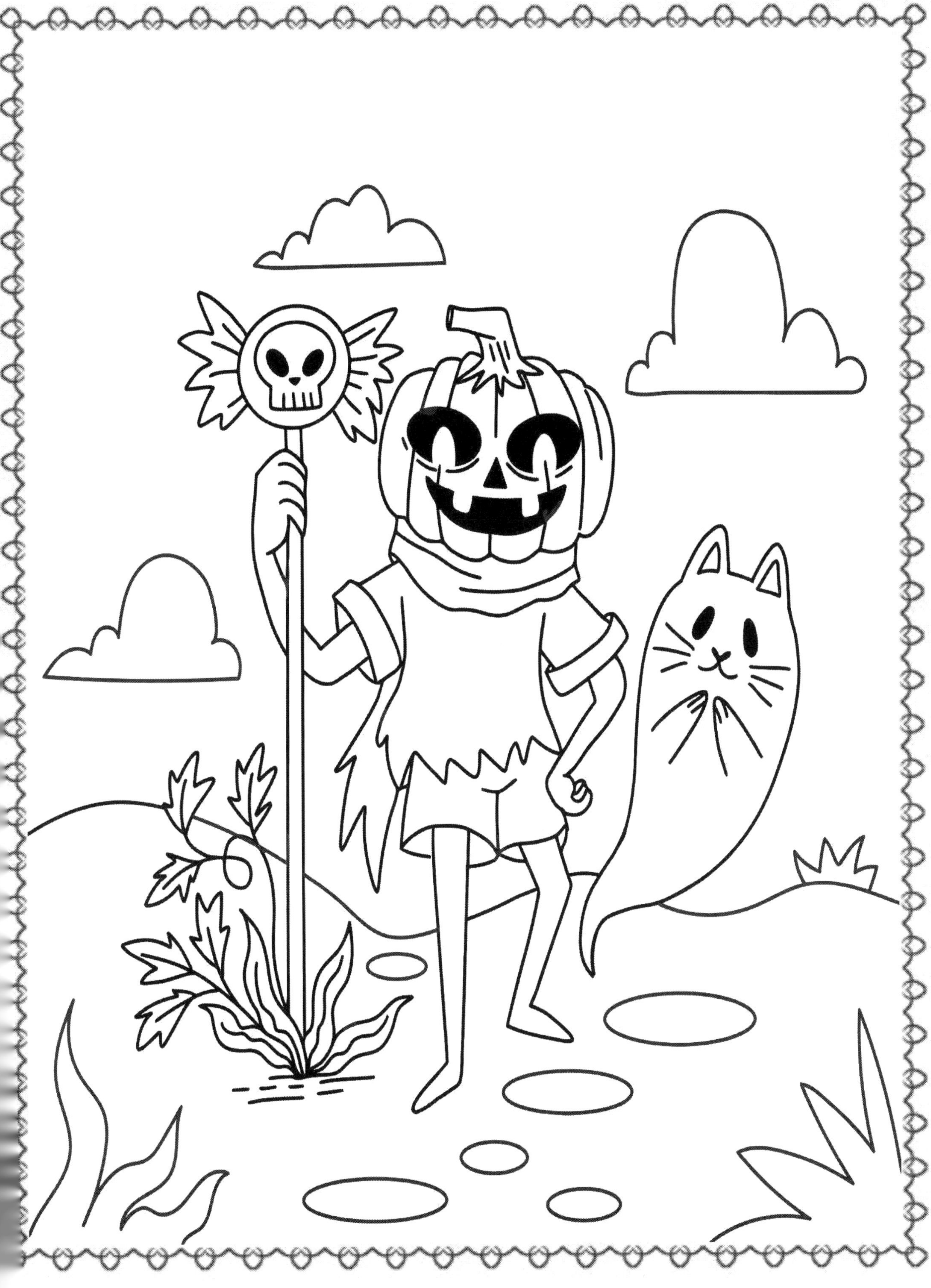

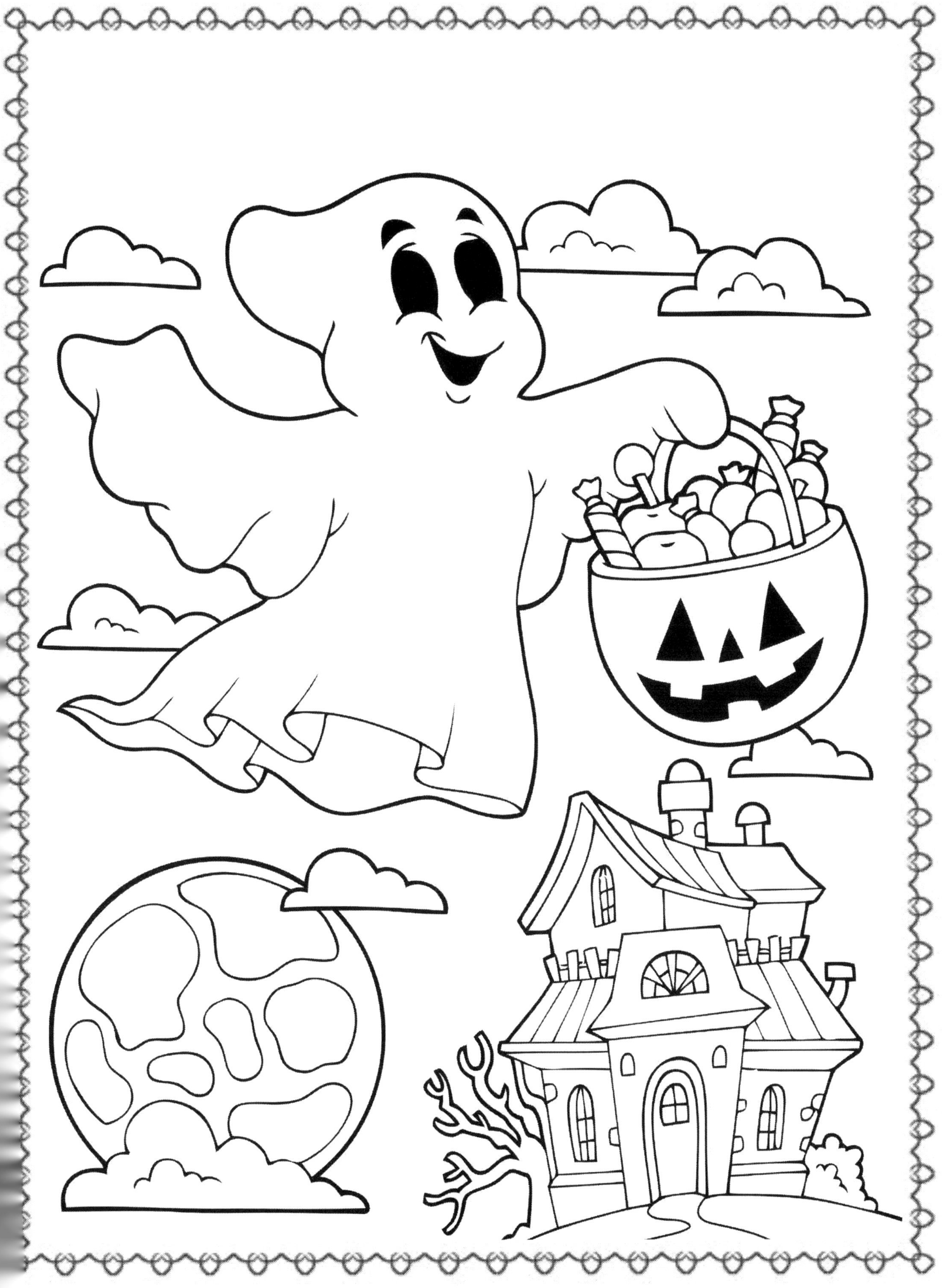

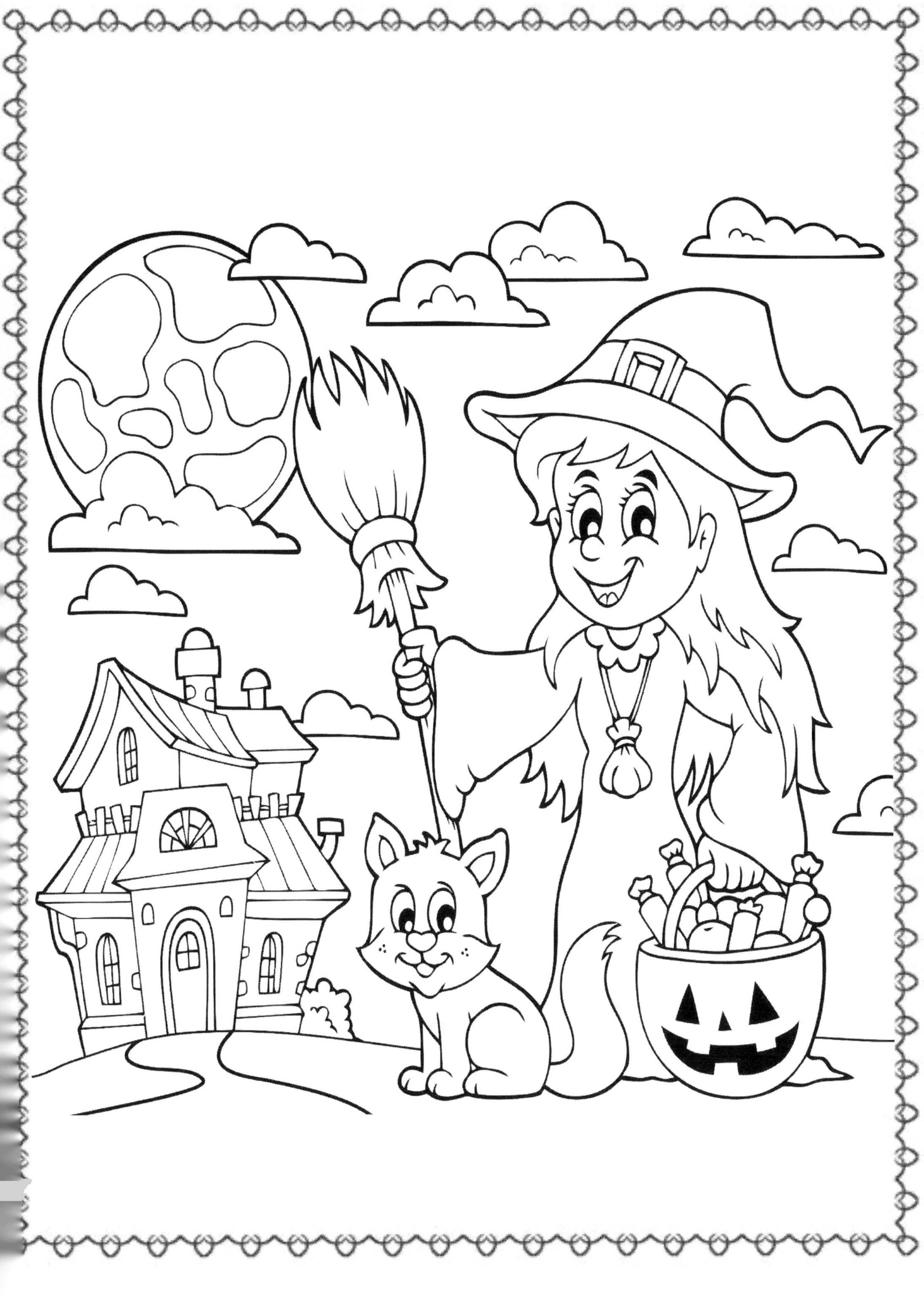

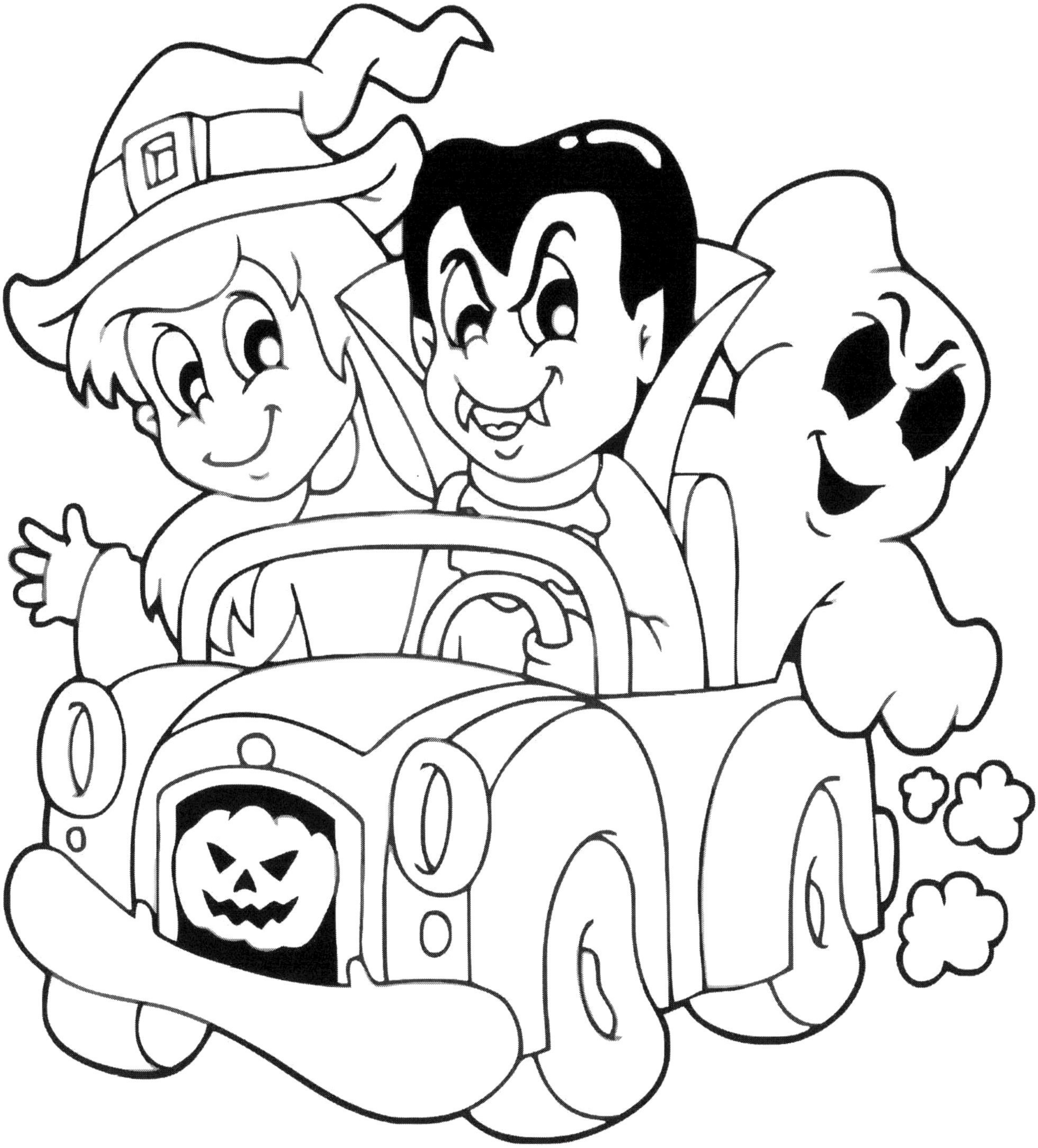

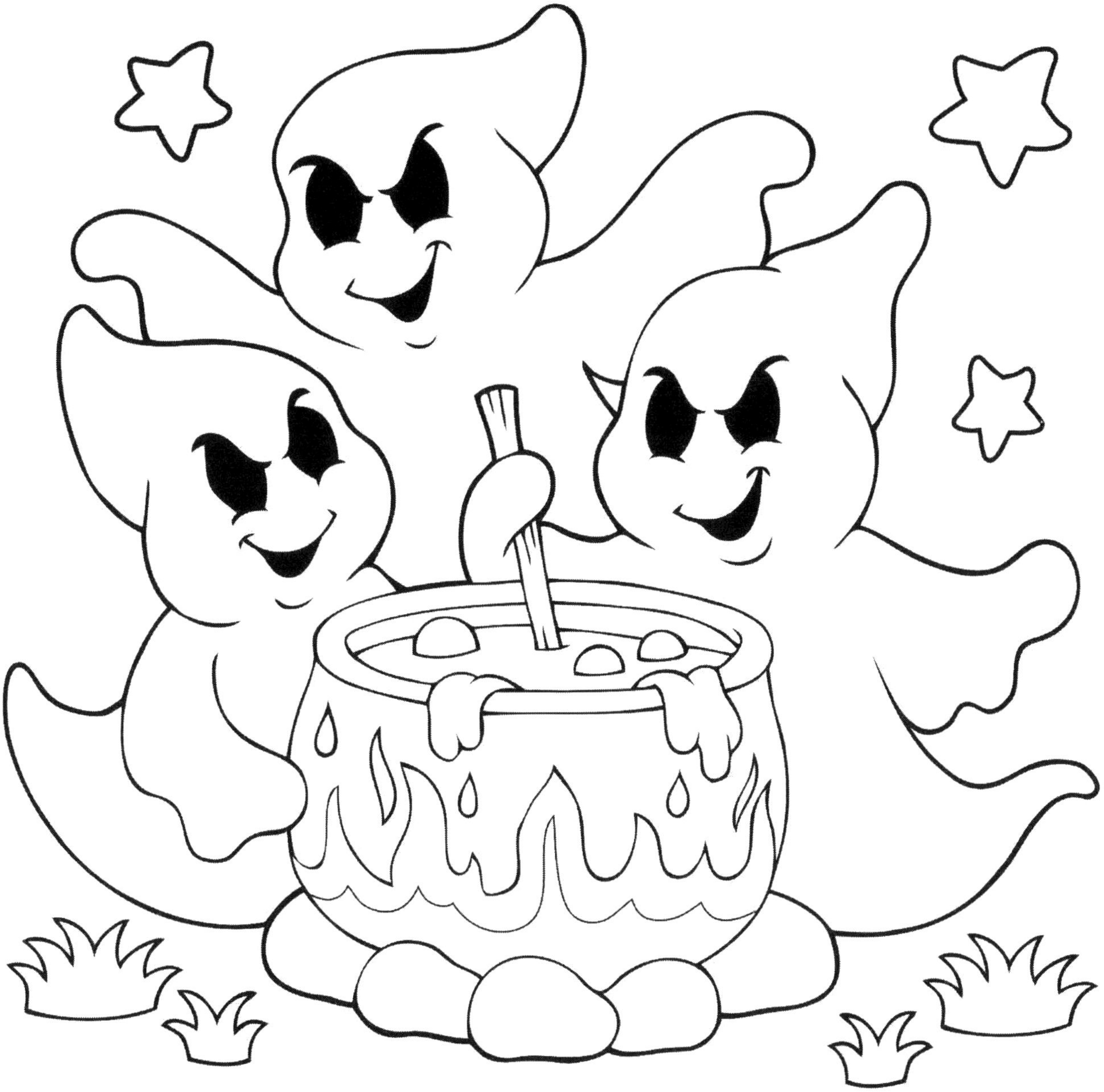

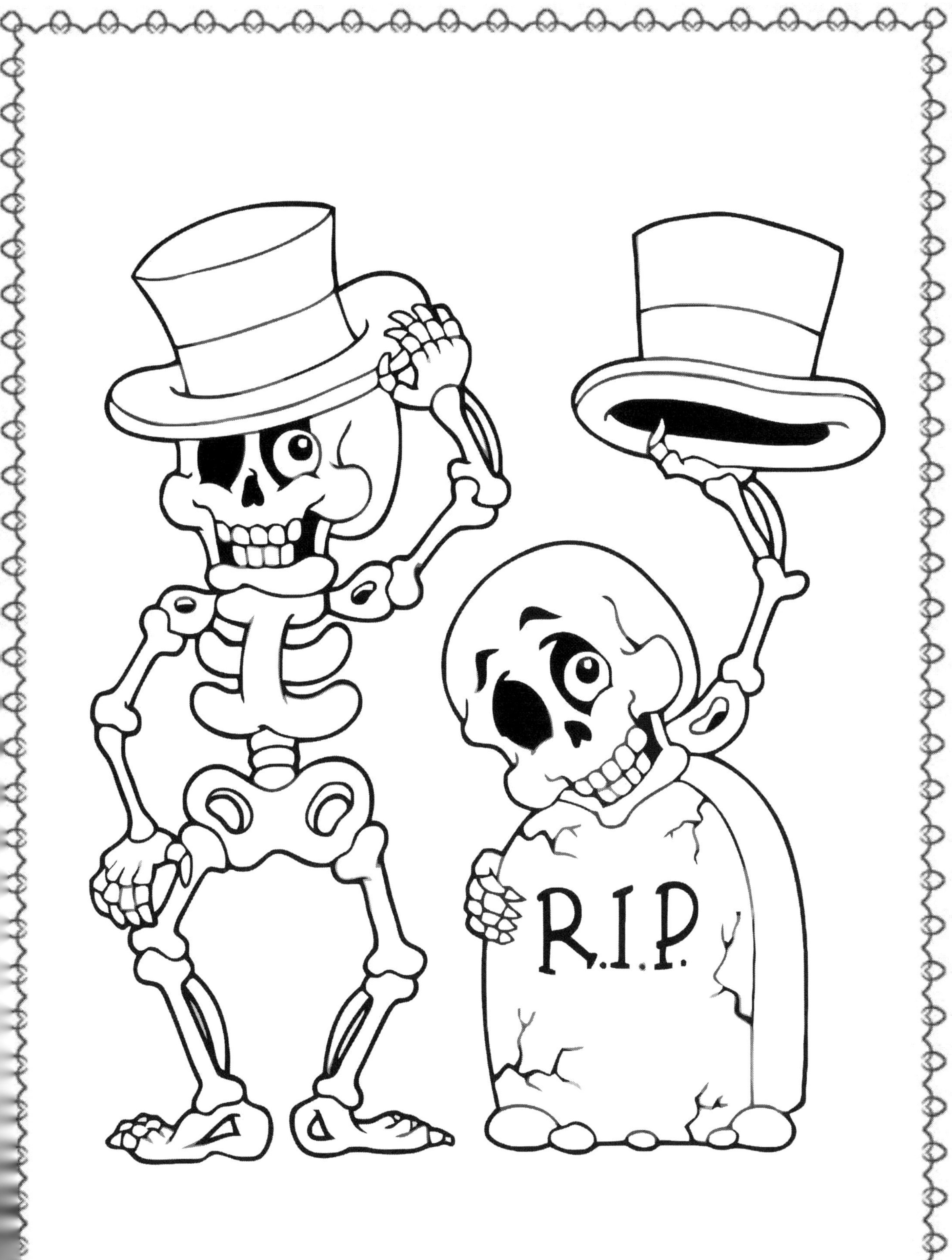
R.I.P.

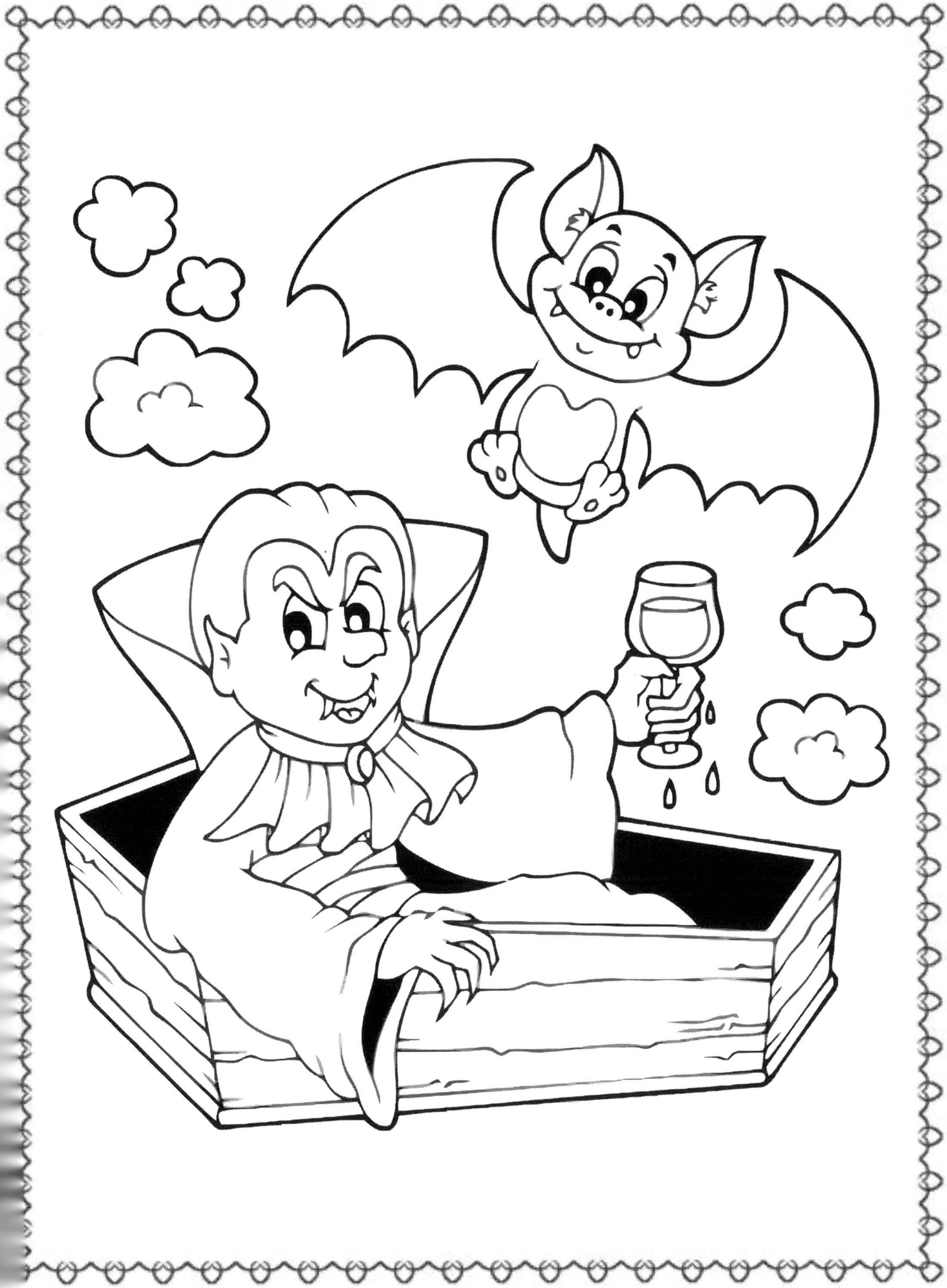

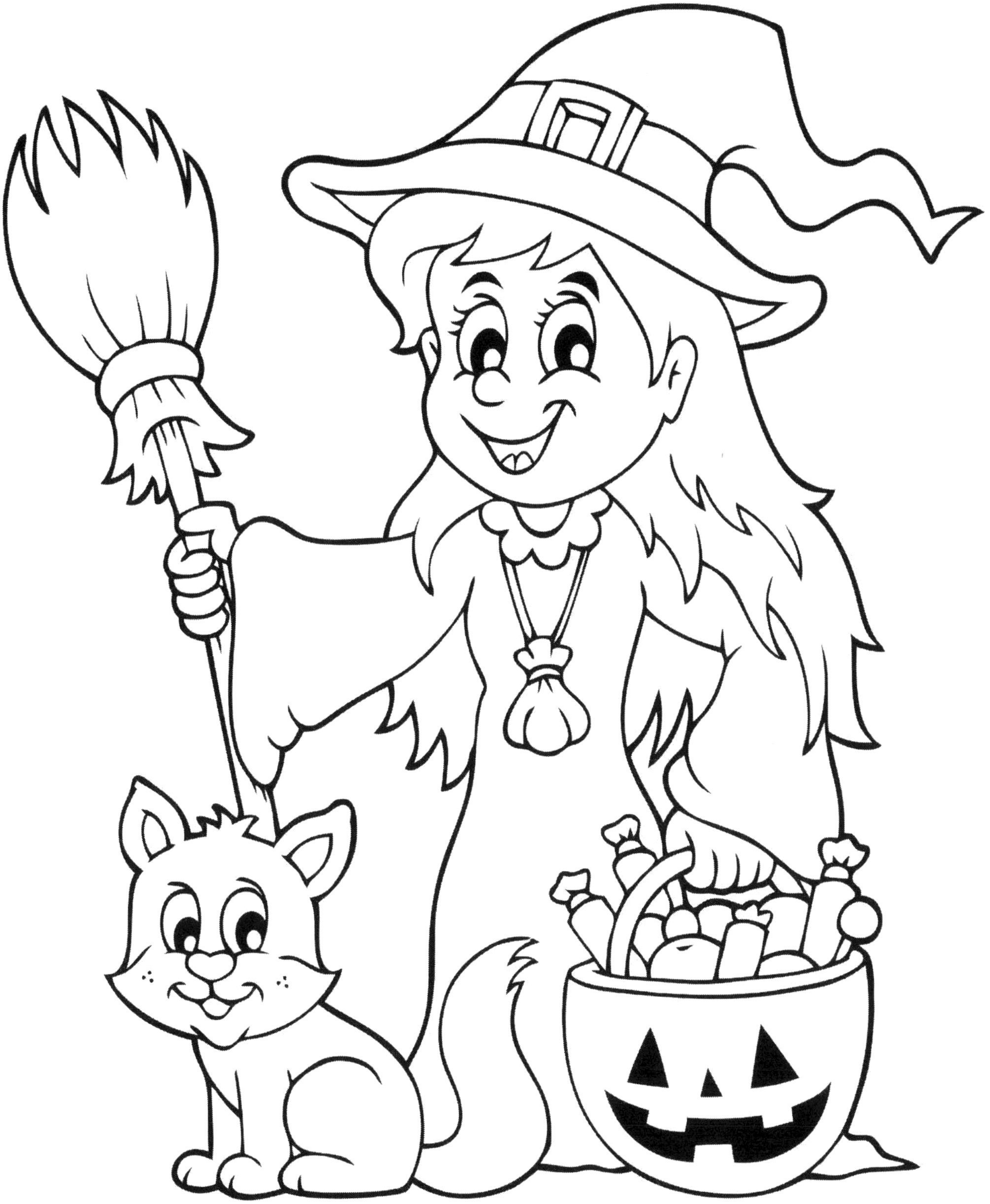

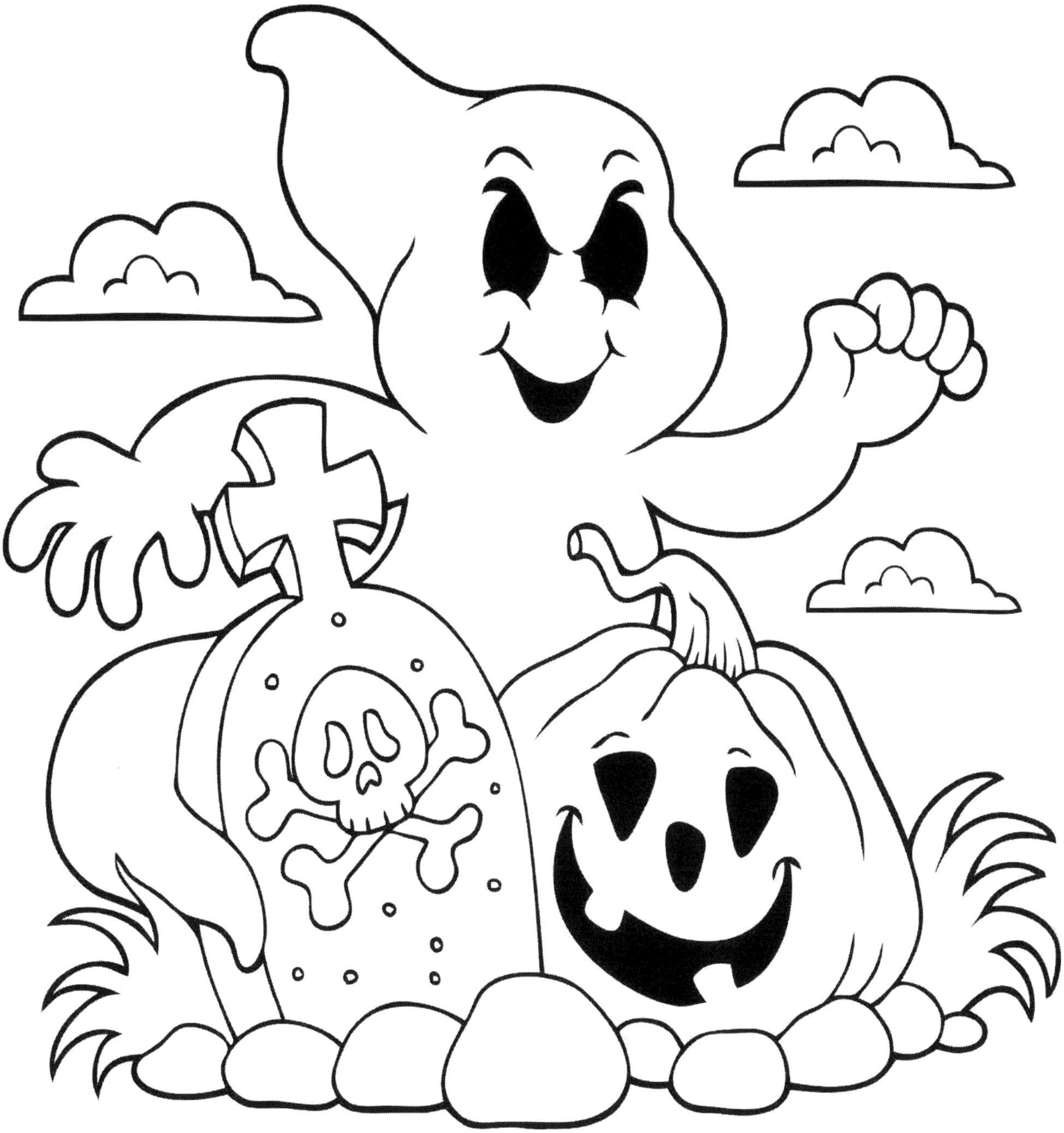

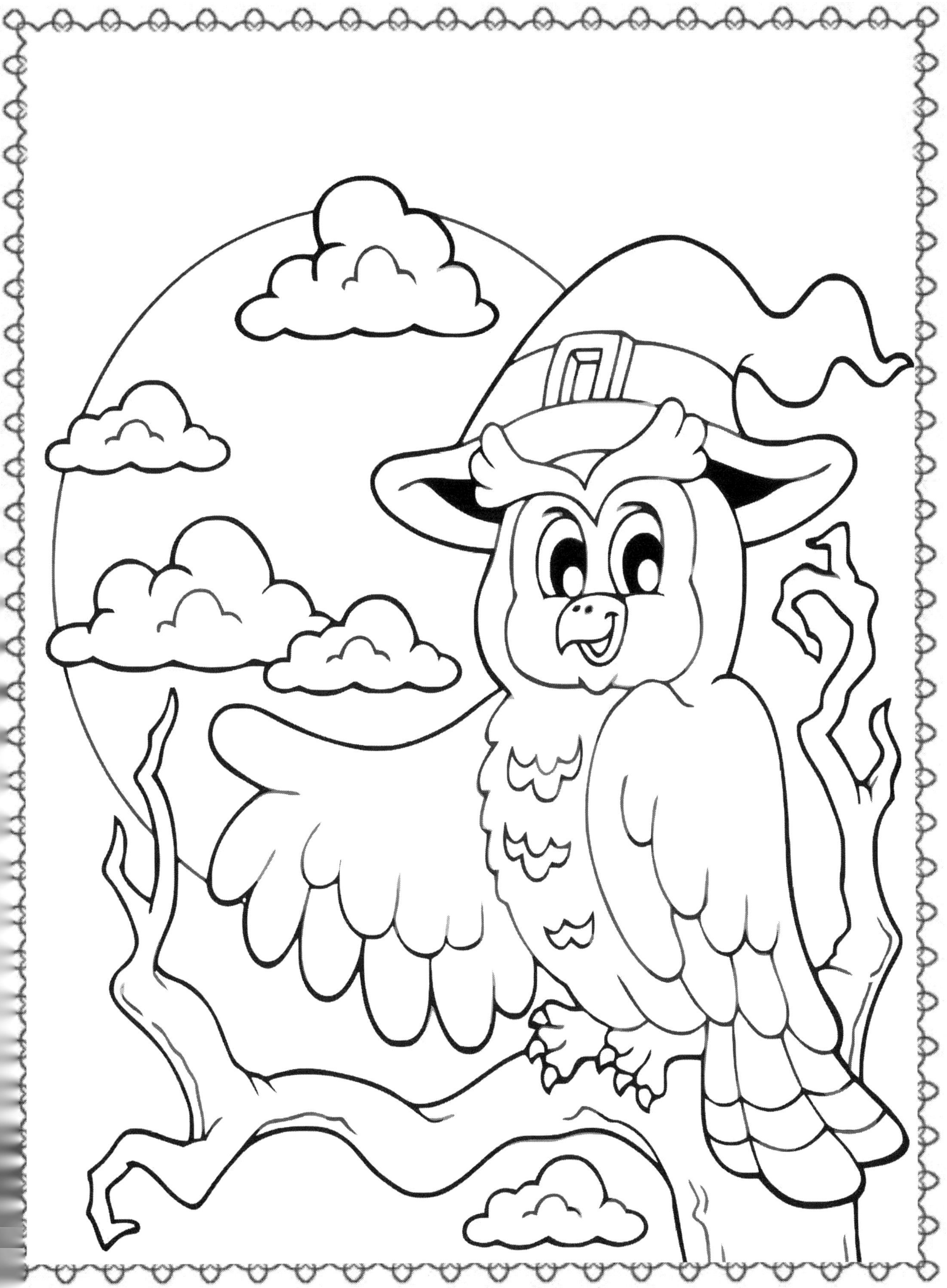

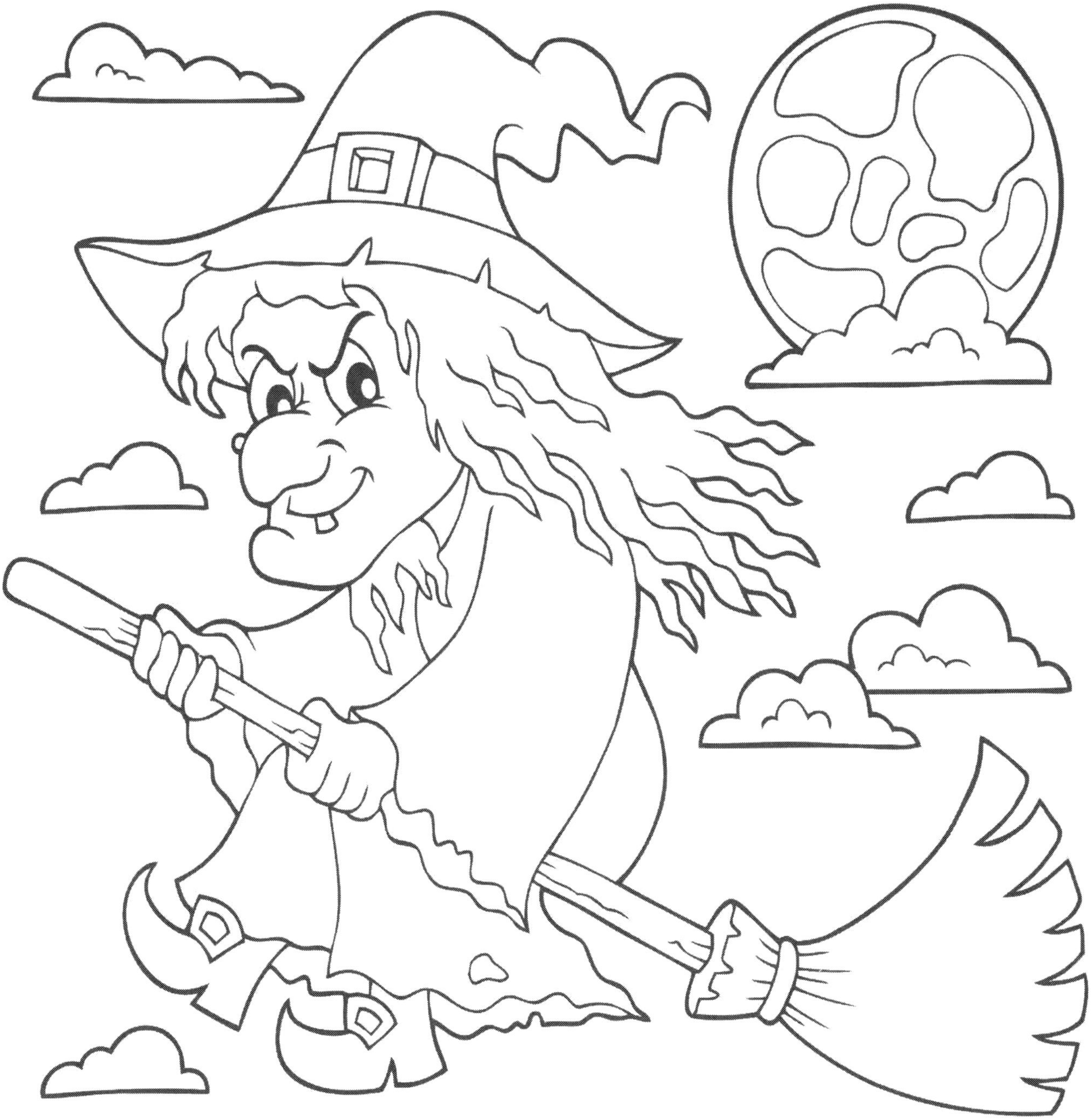

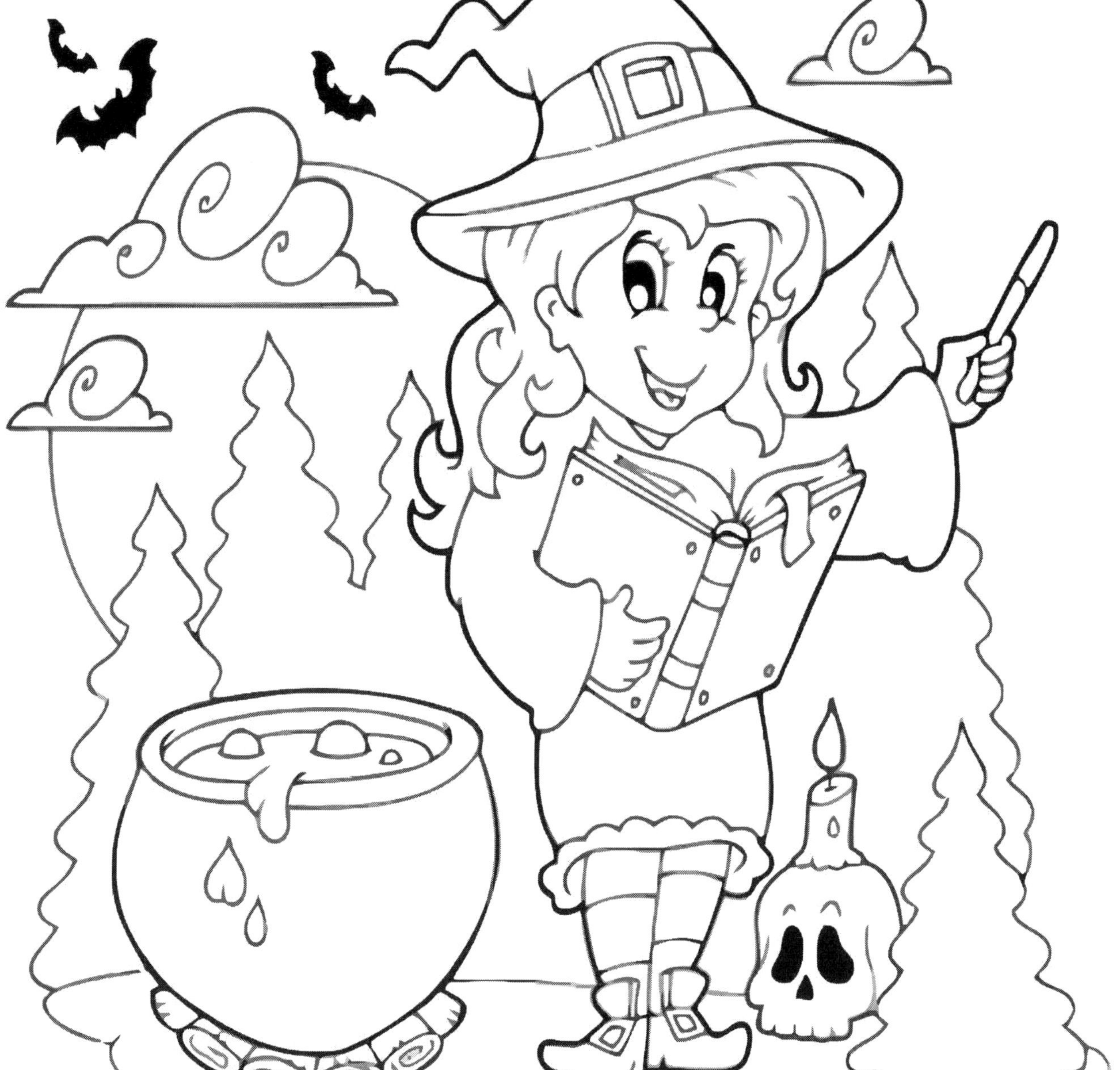

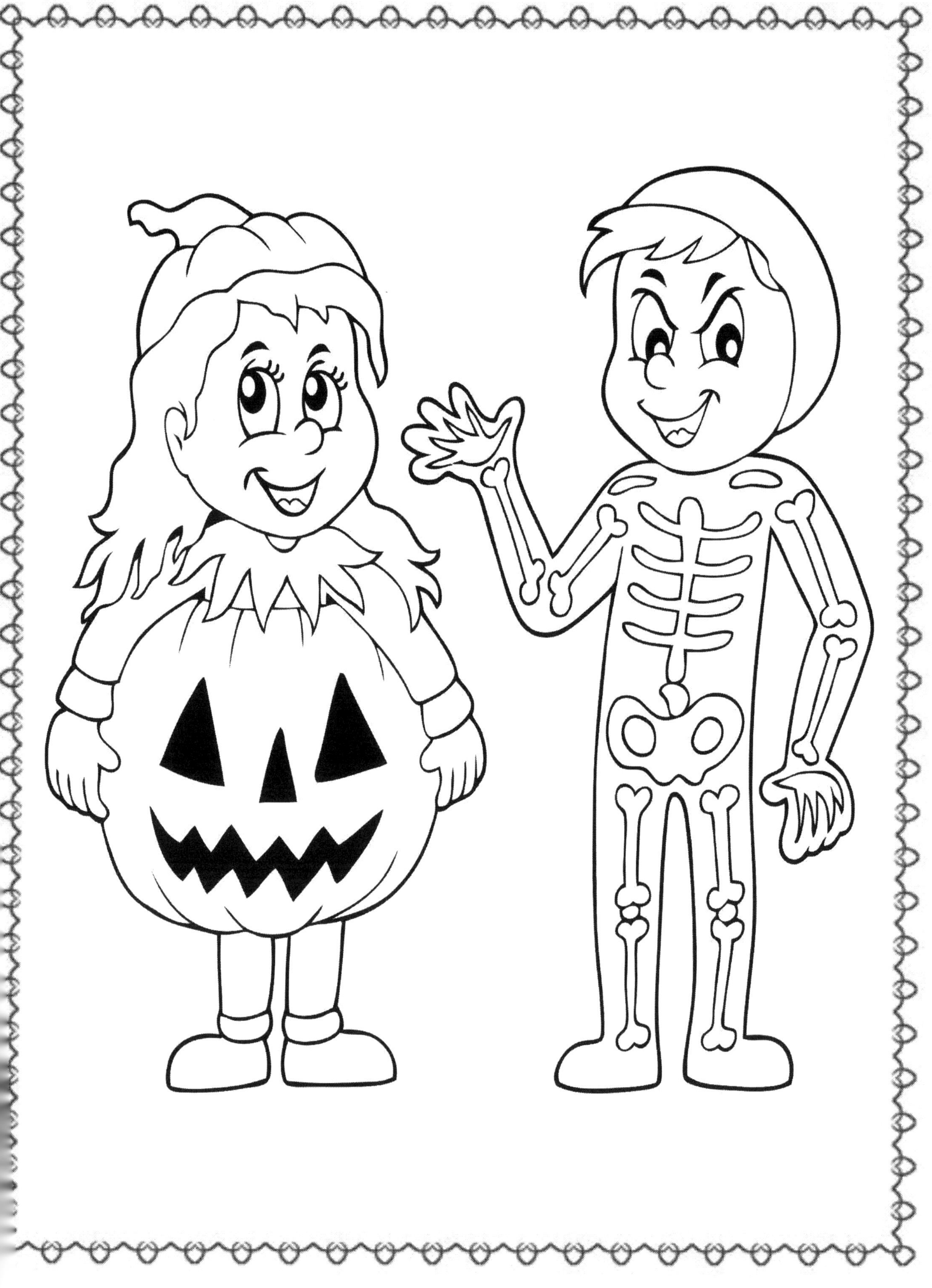

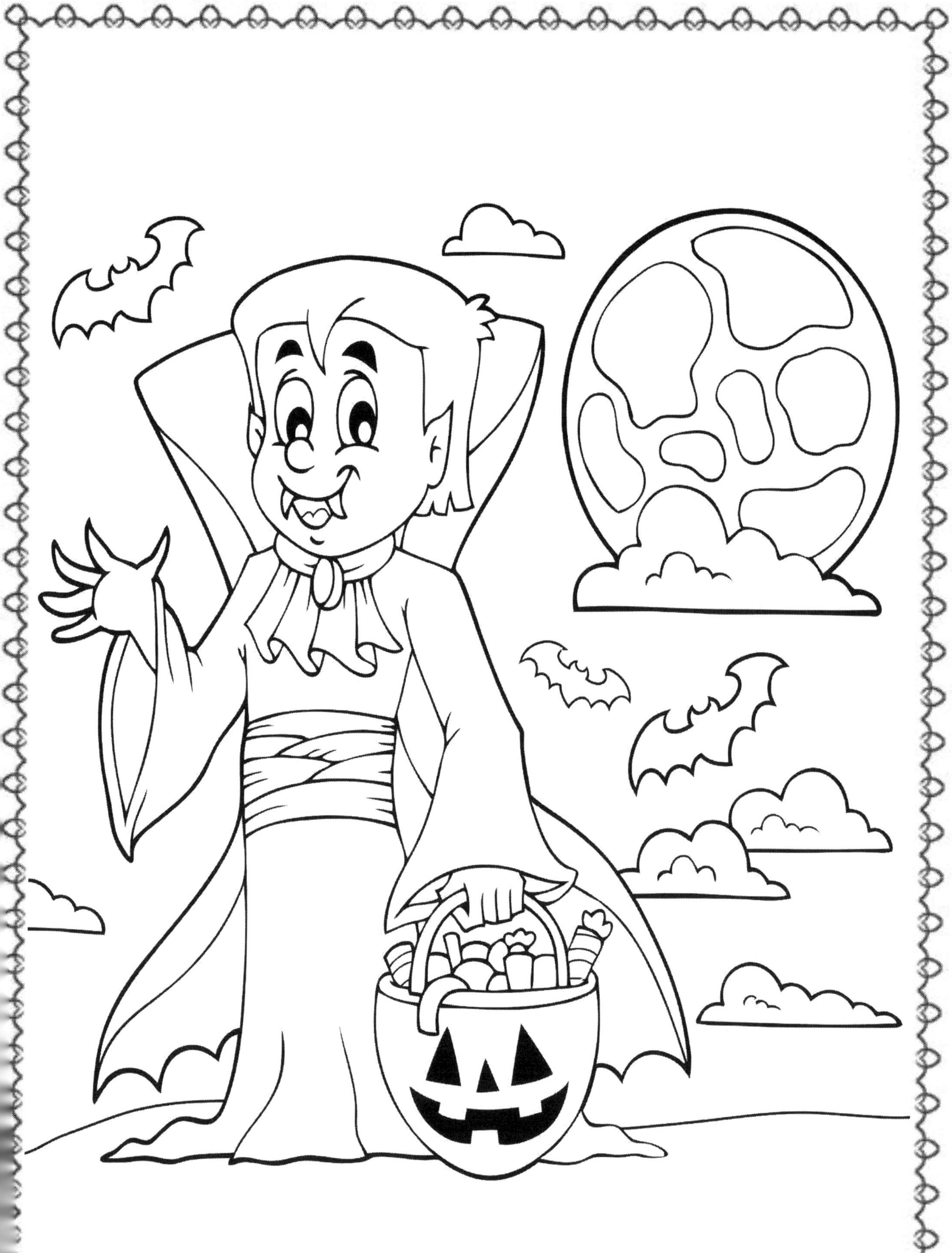

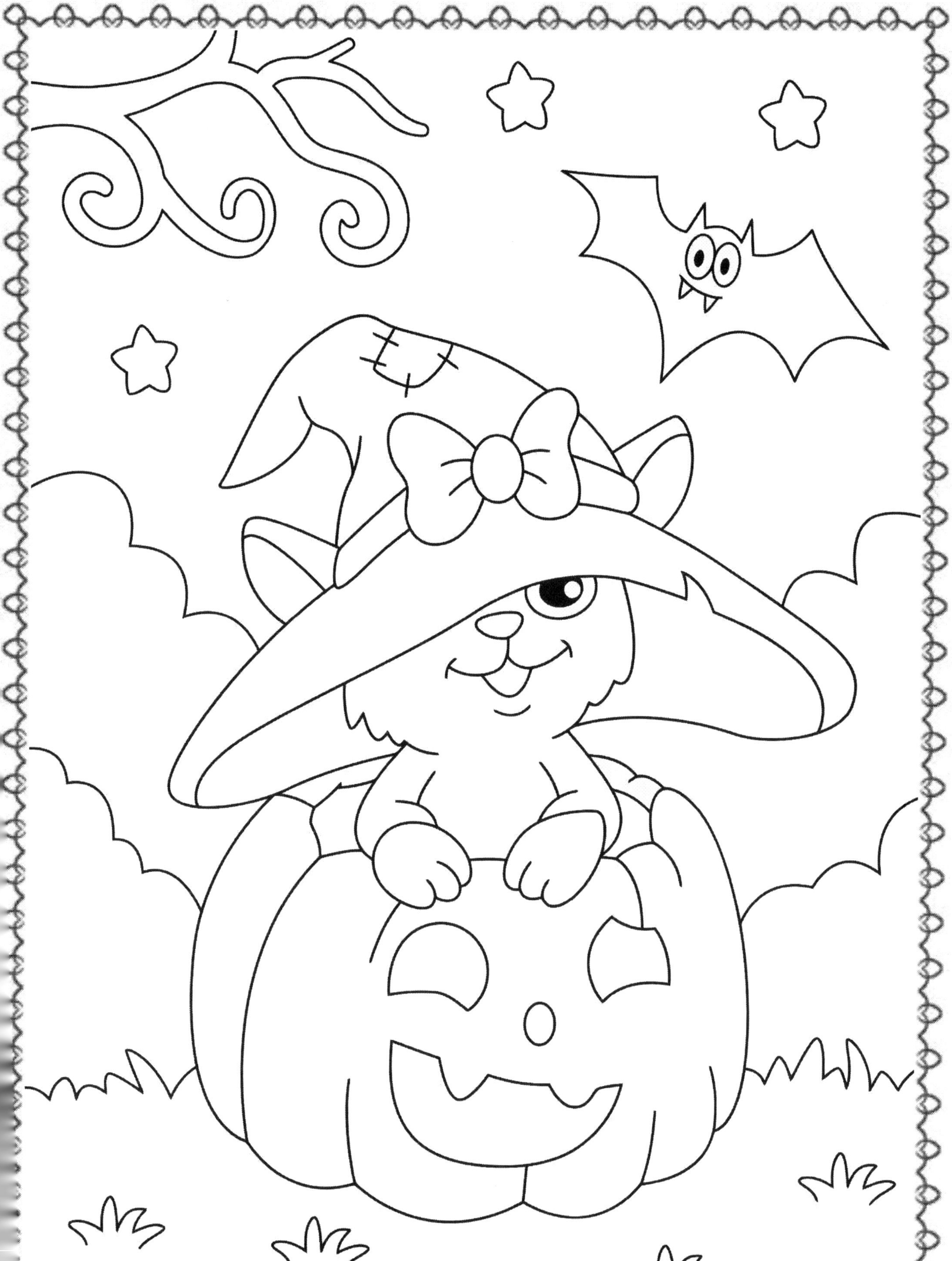

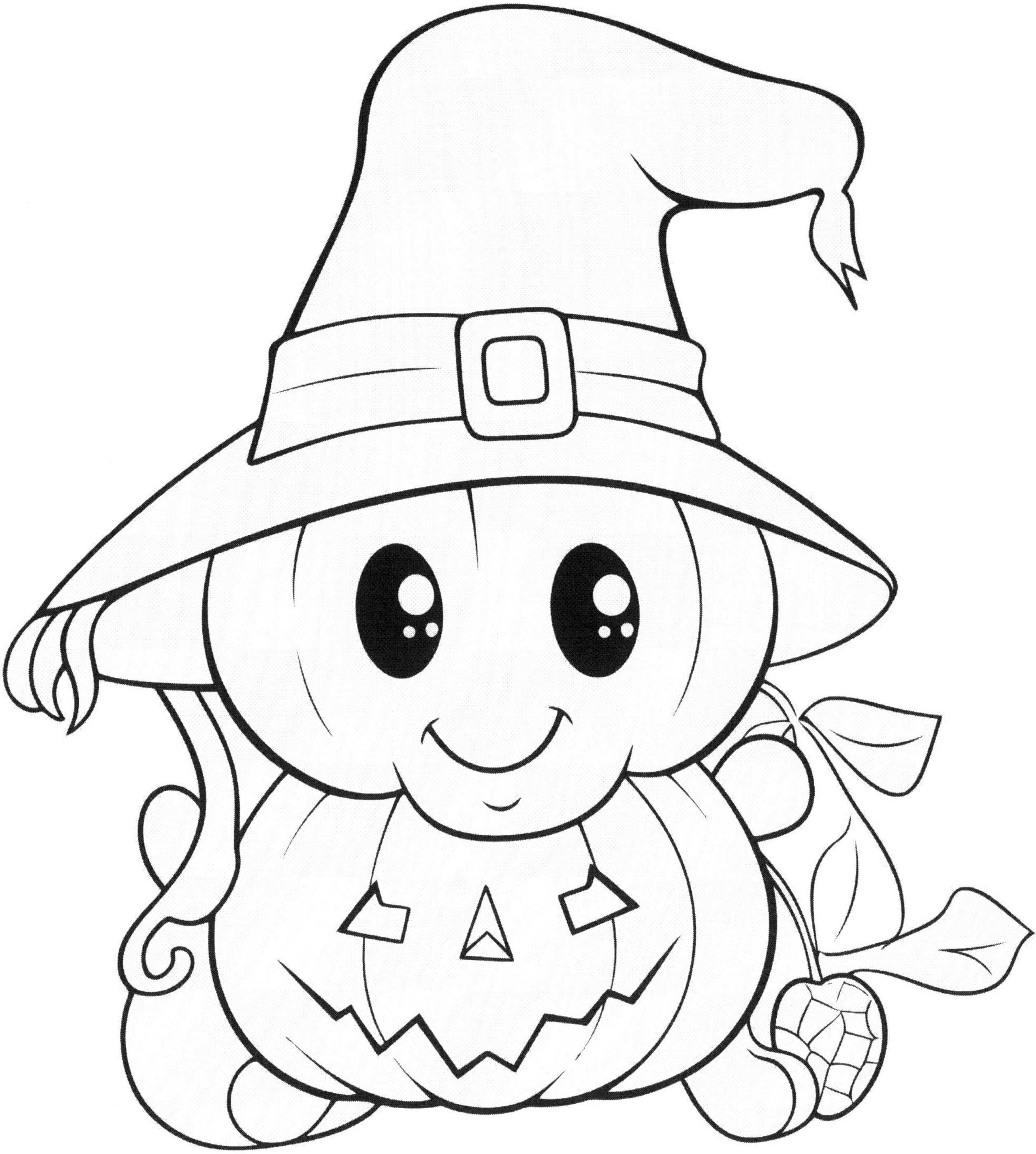

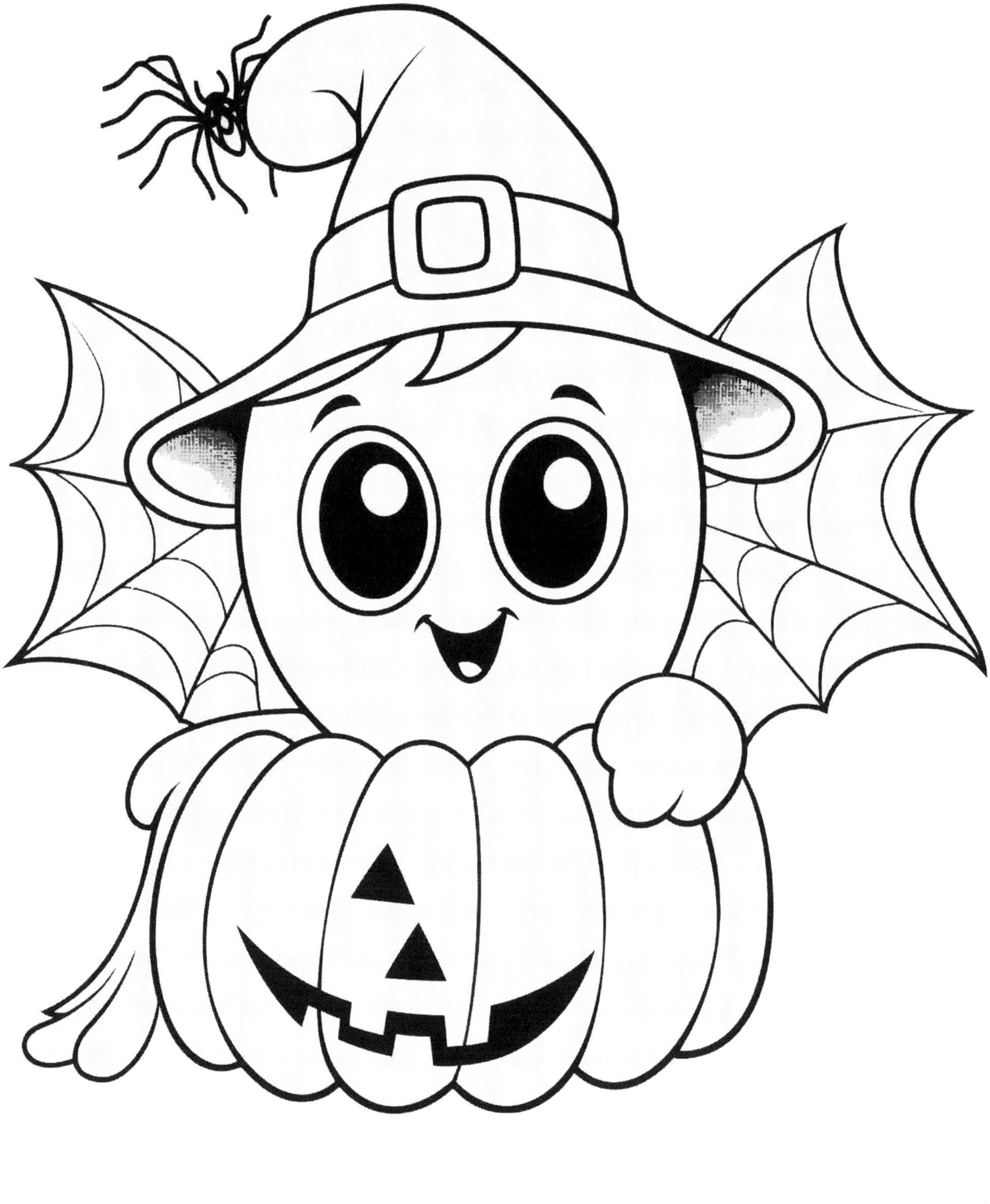

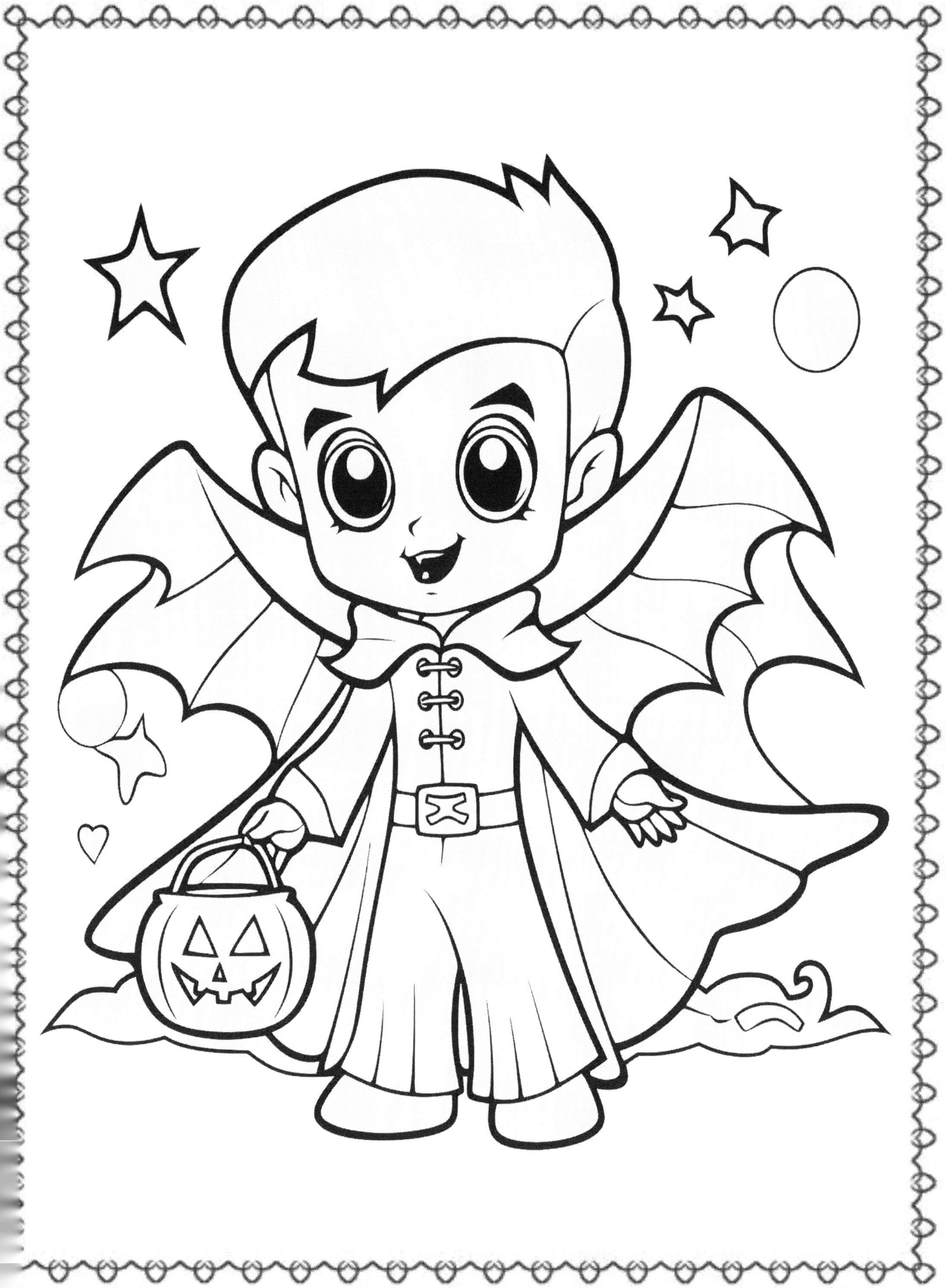

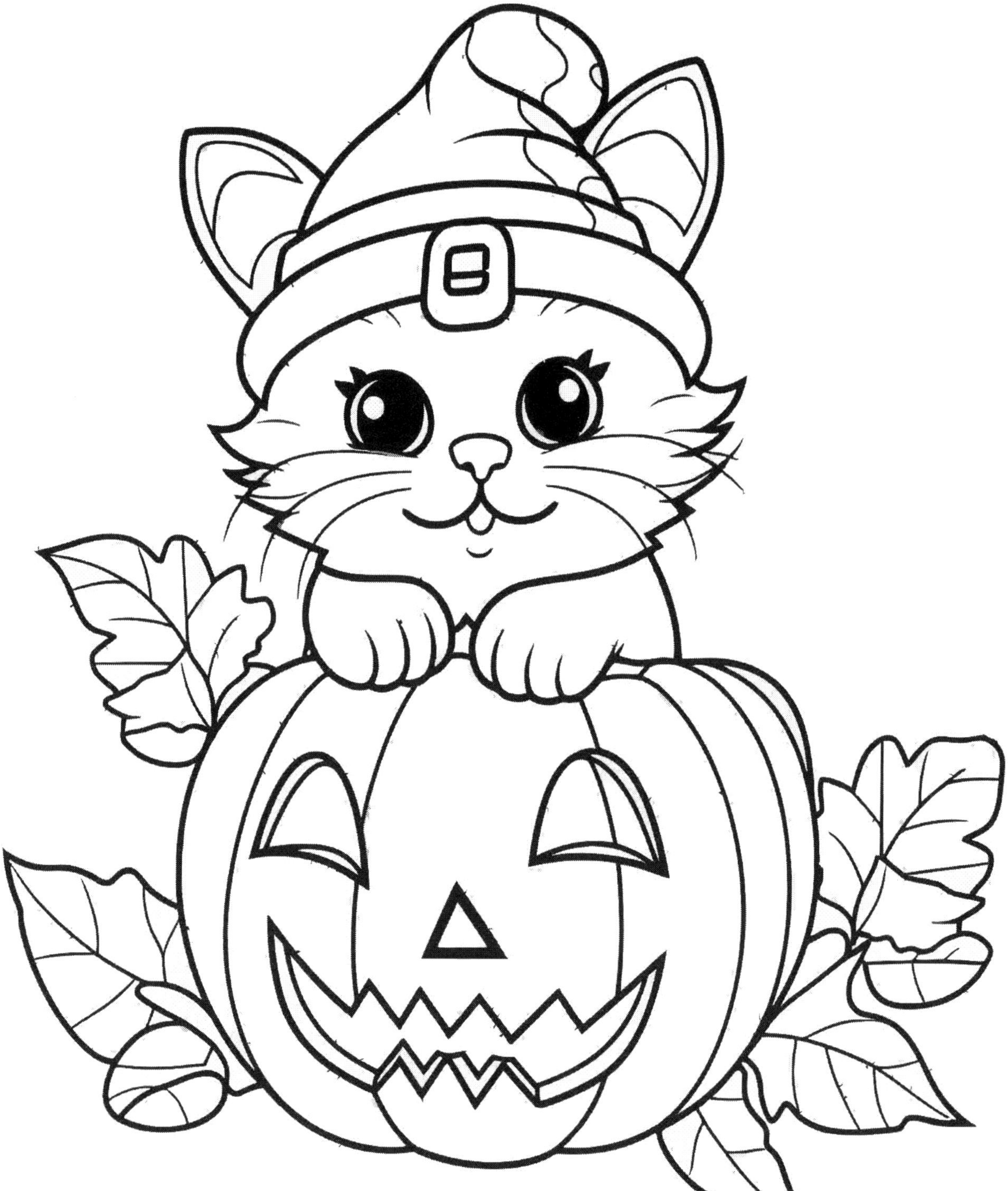

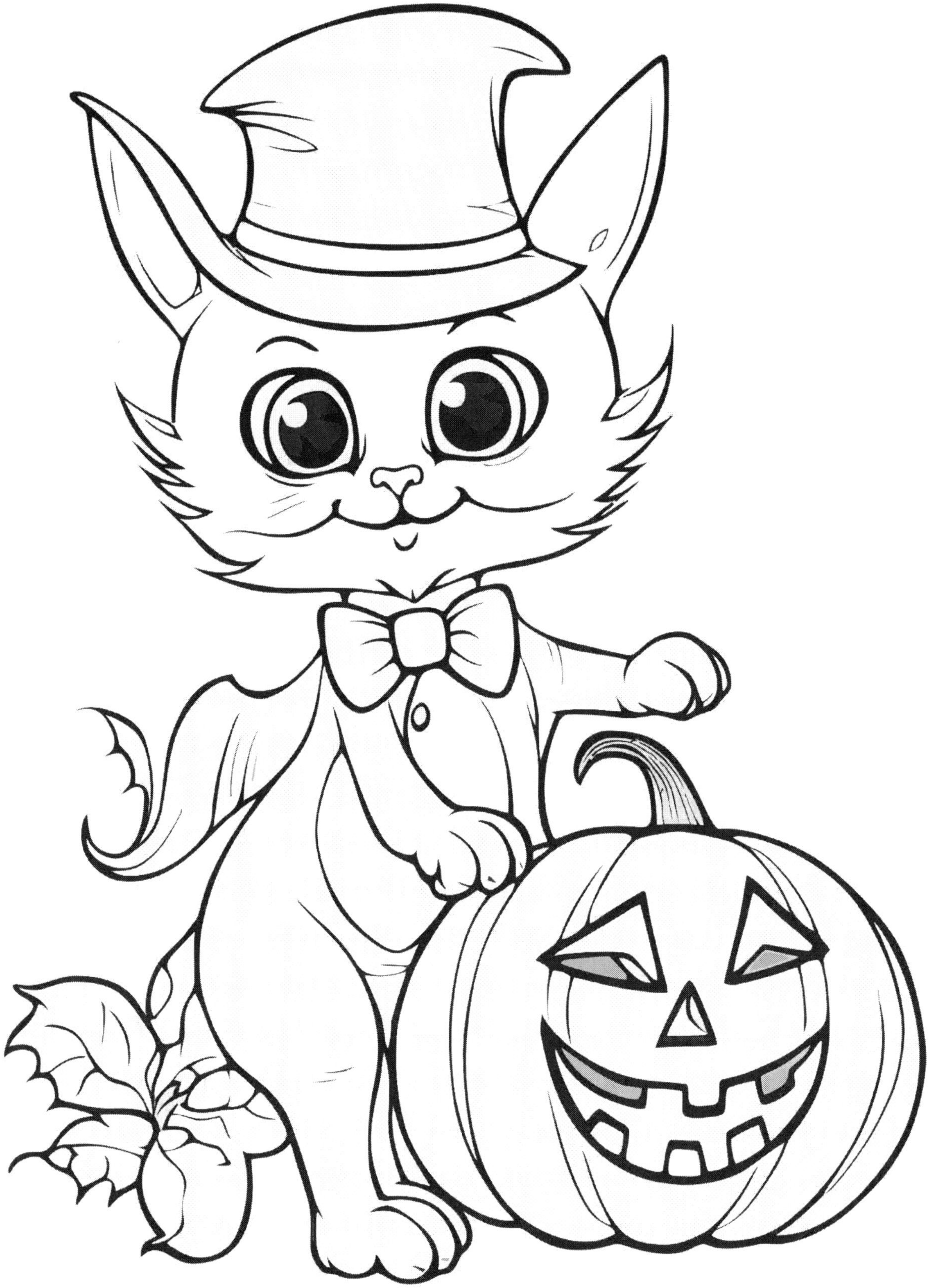

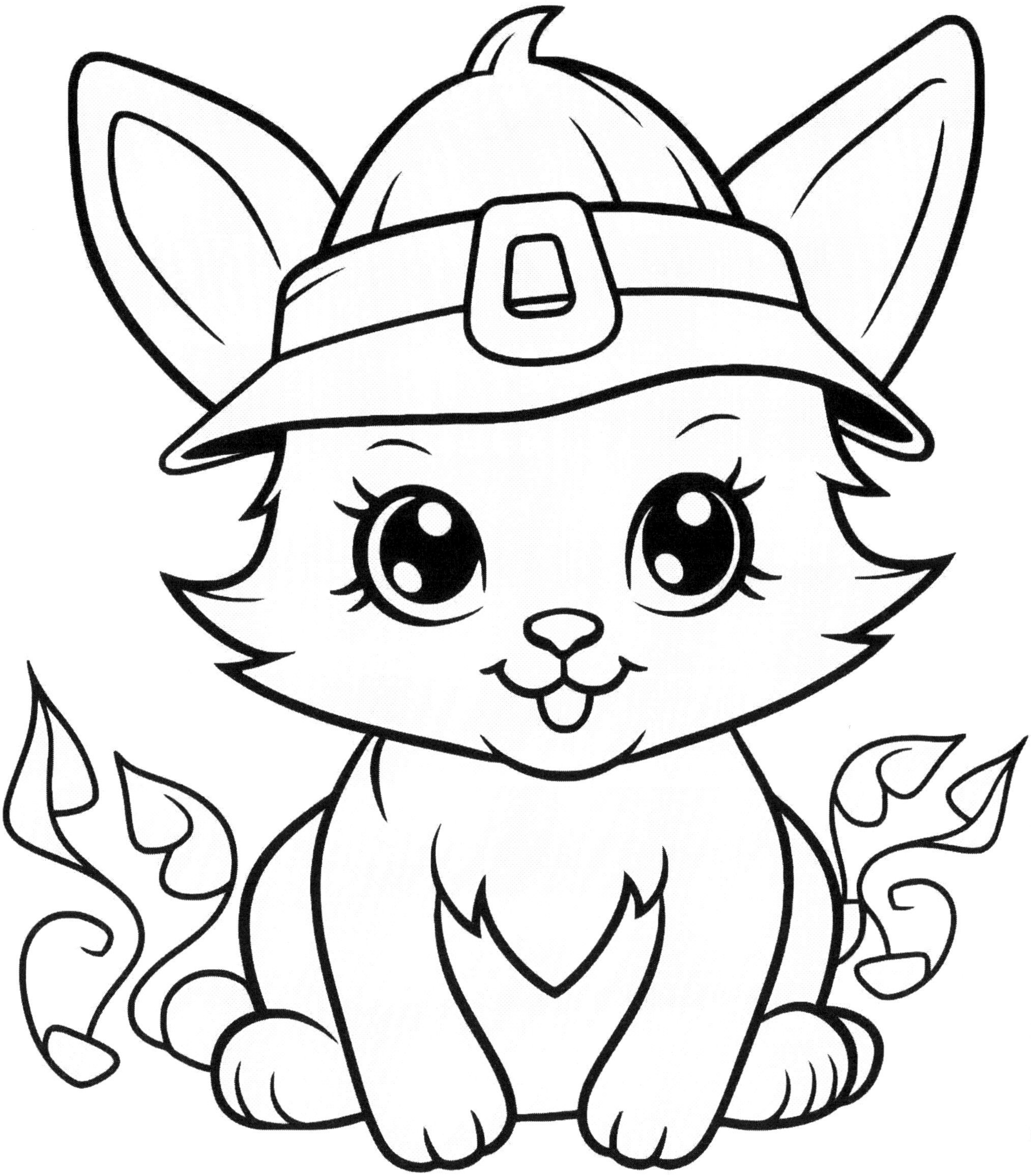

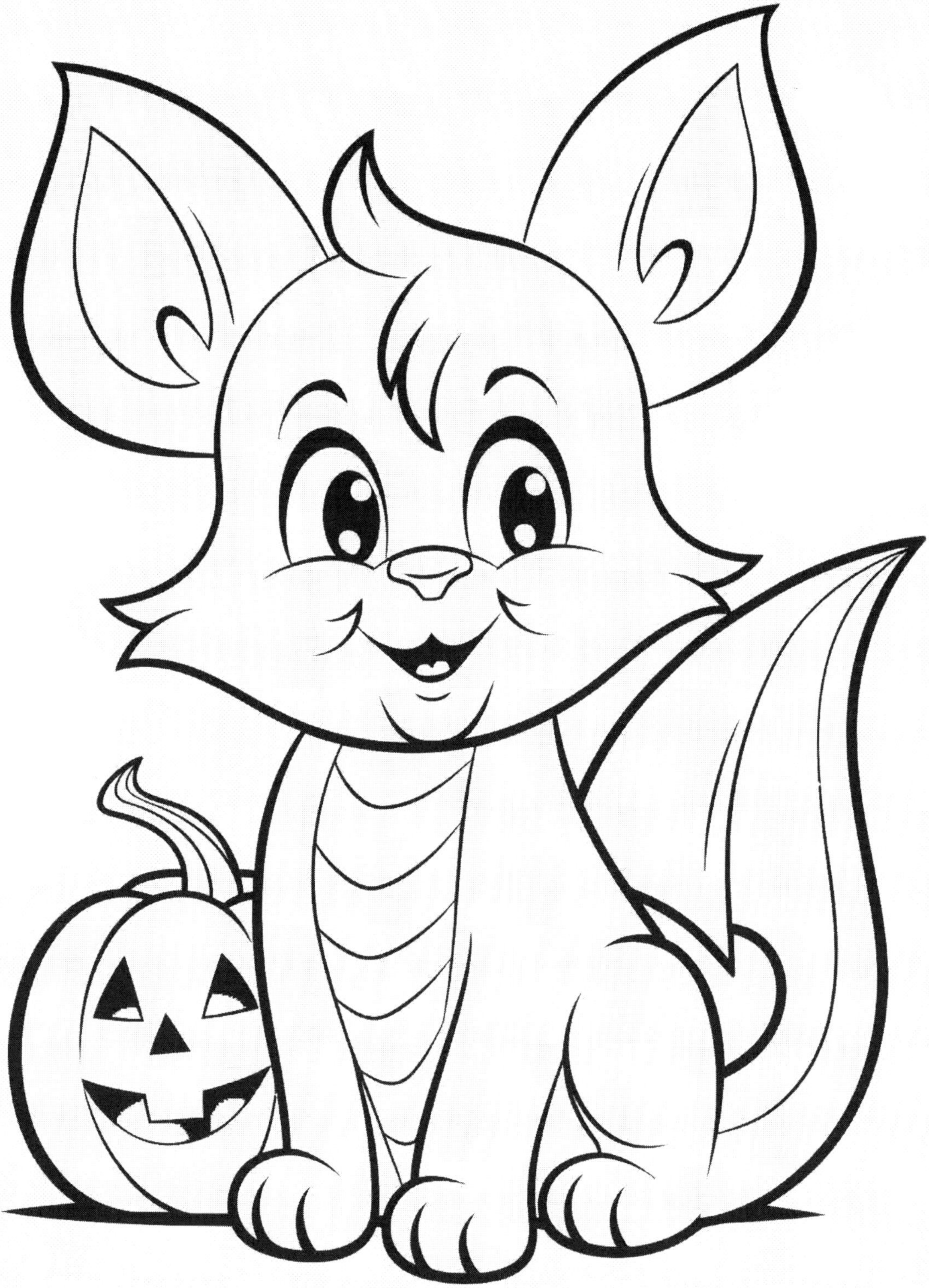

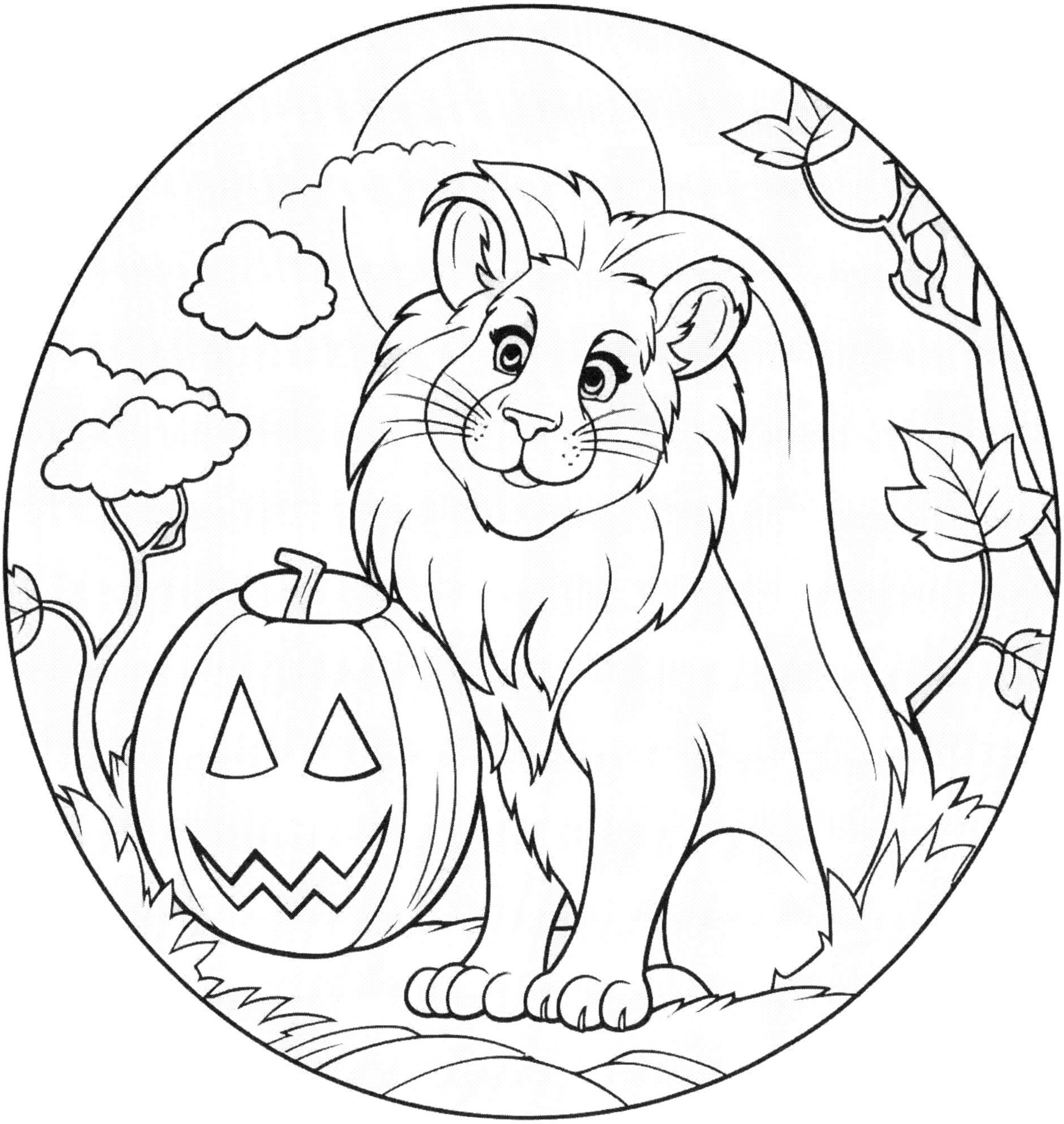

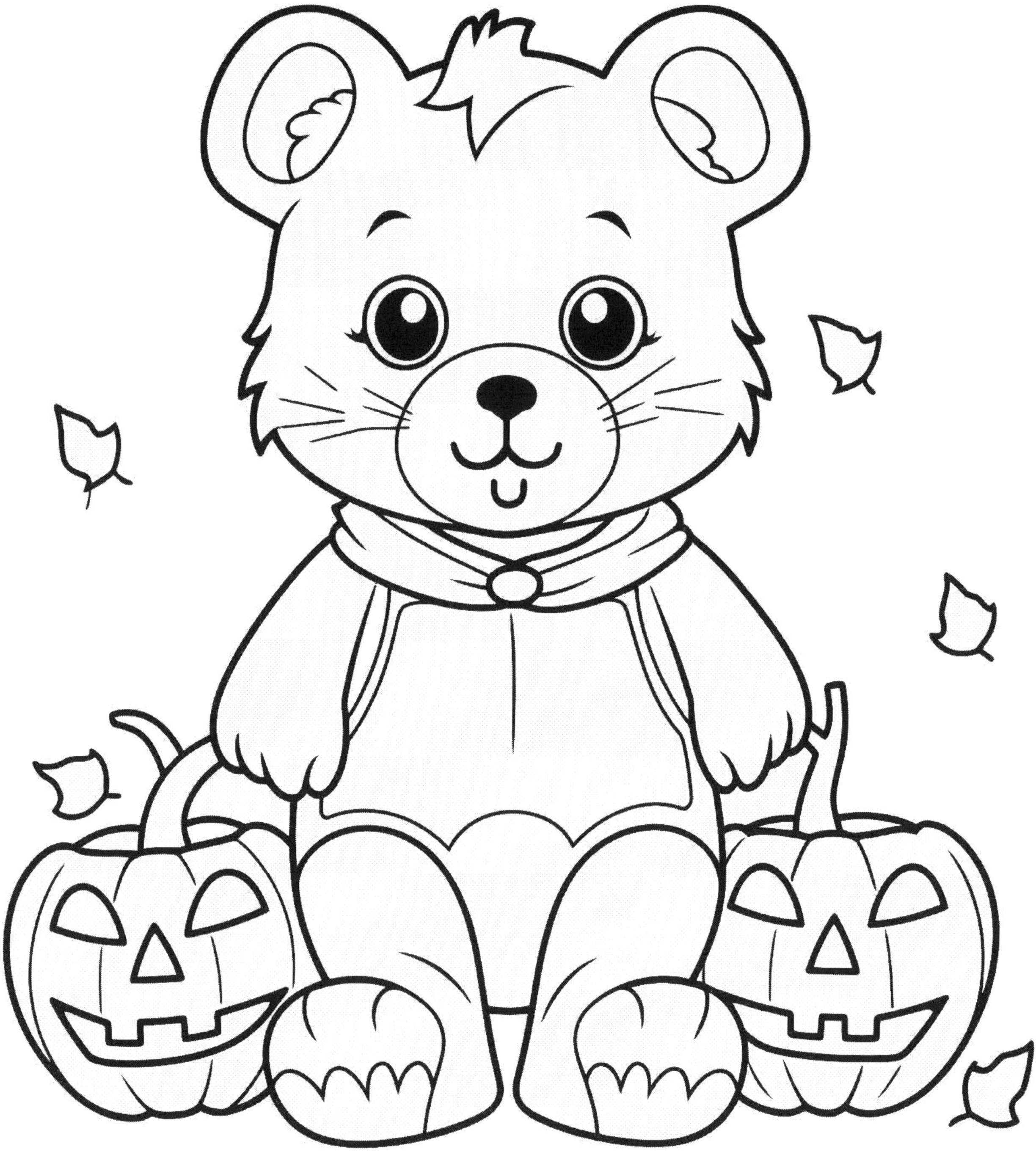

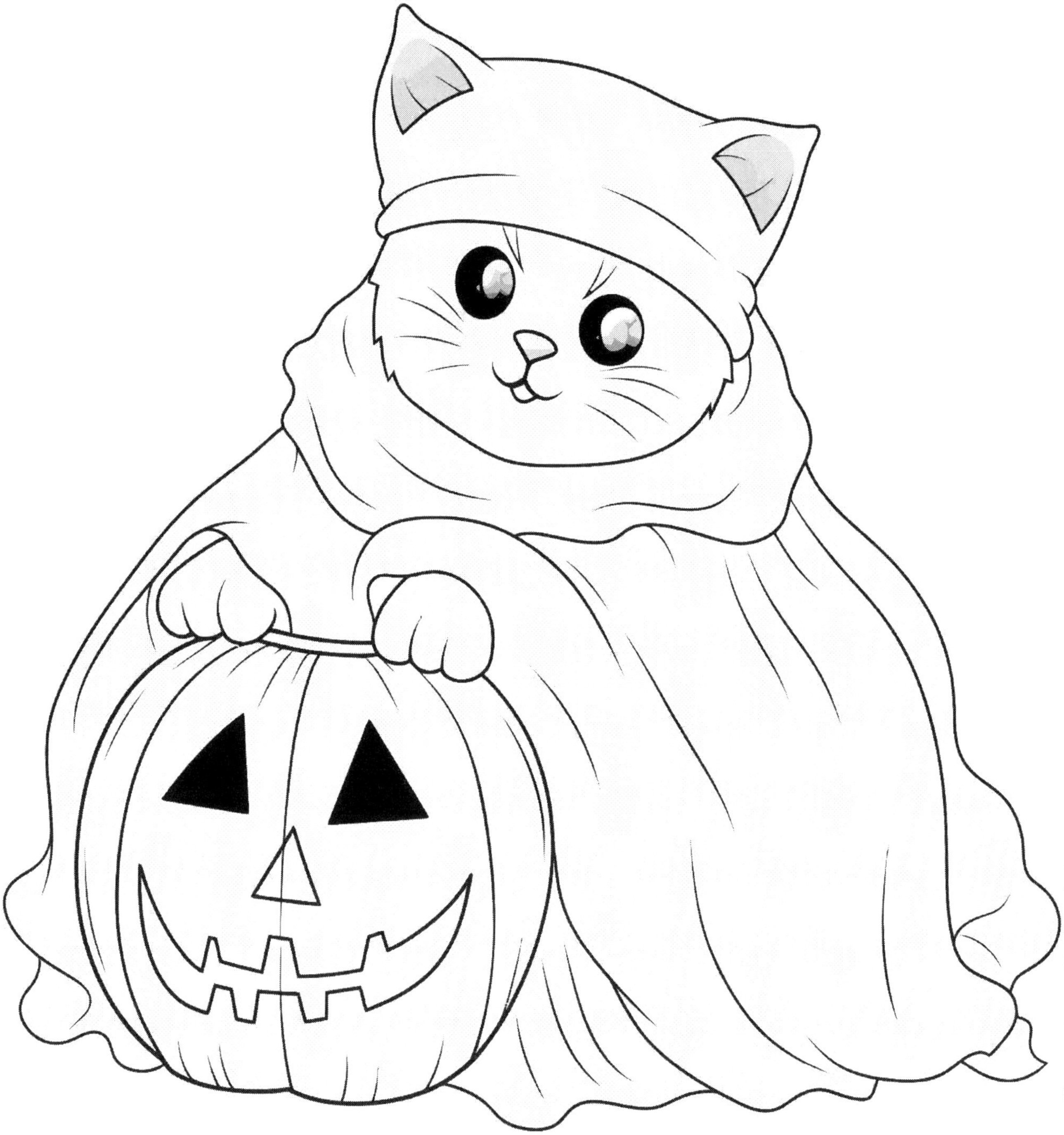

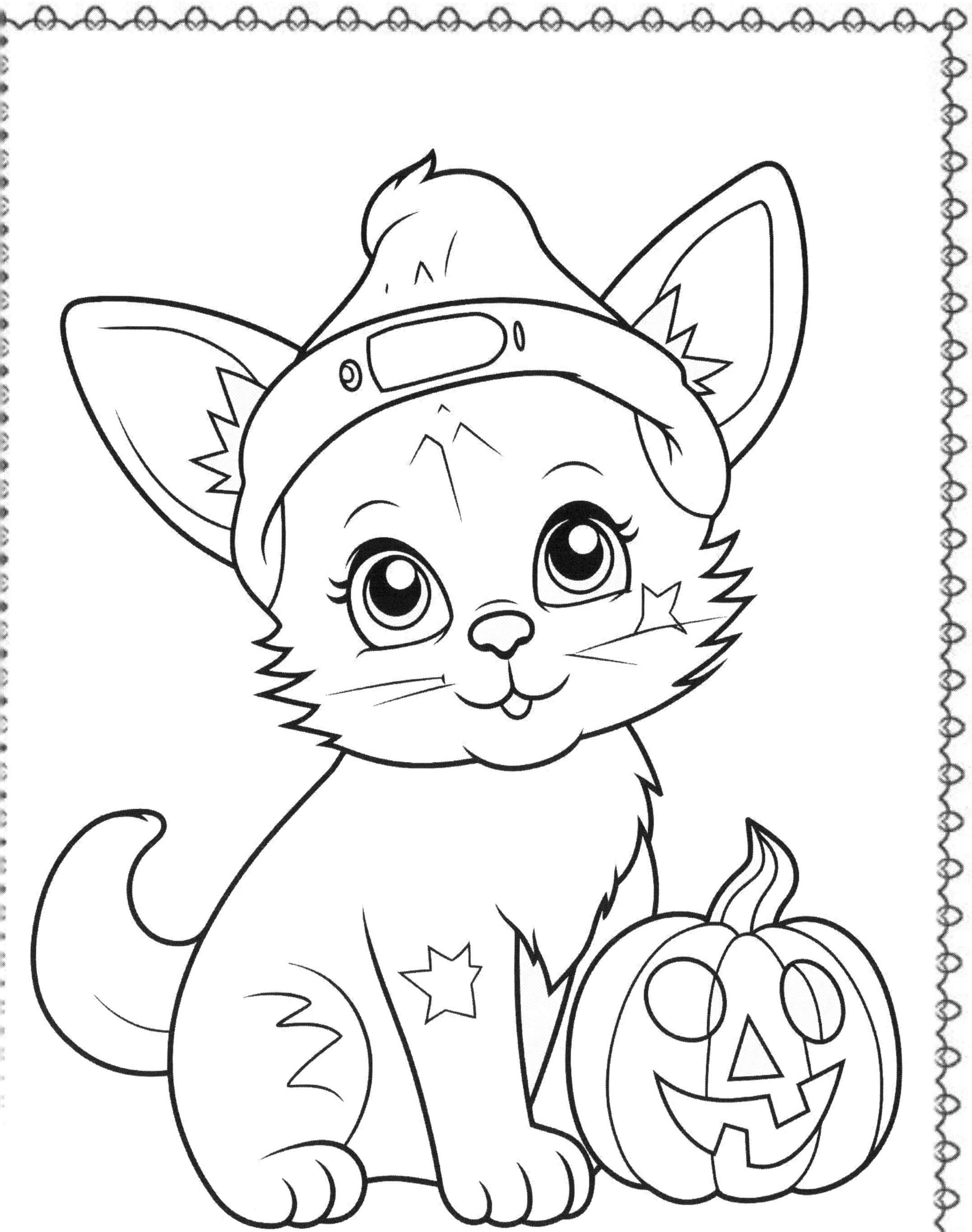

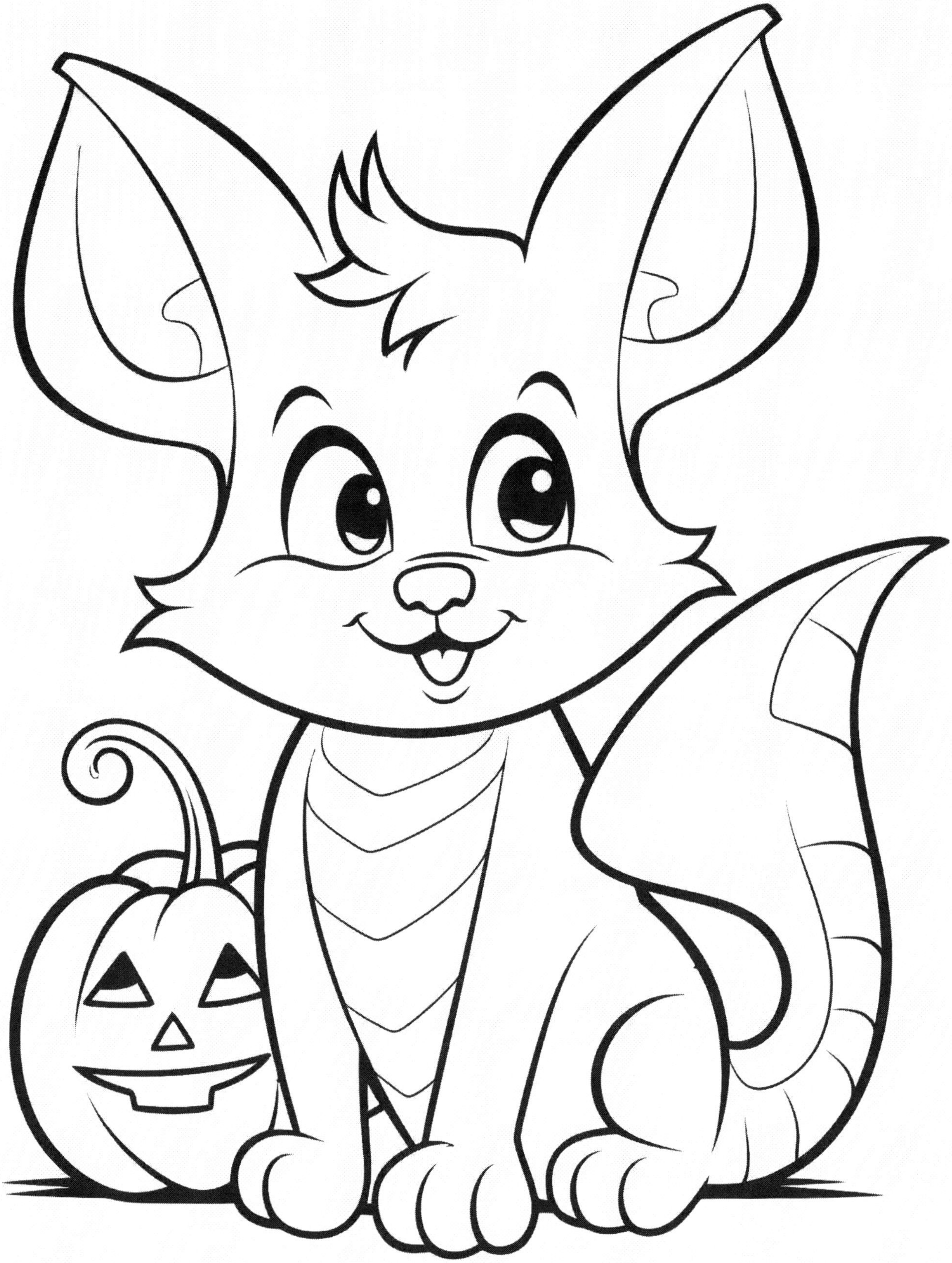

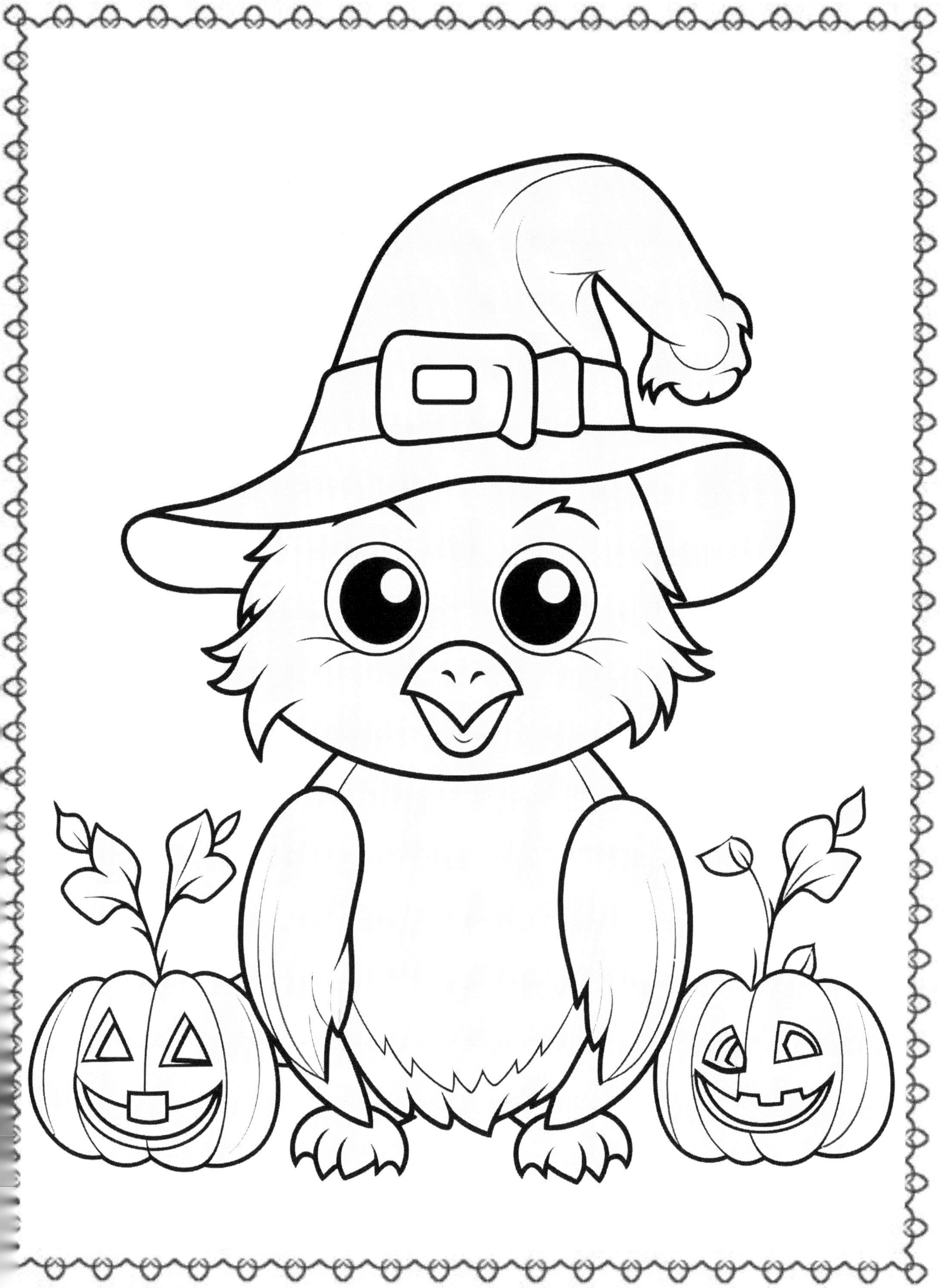

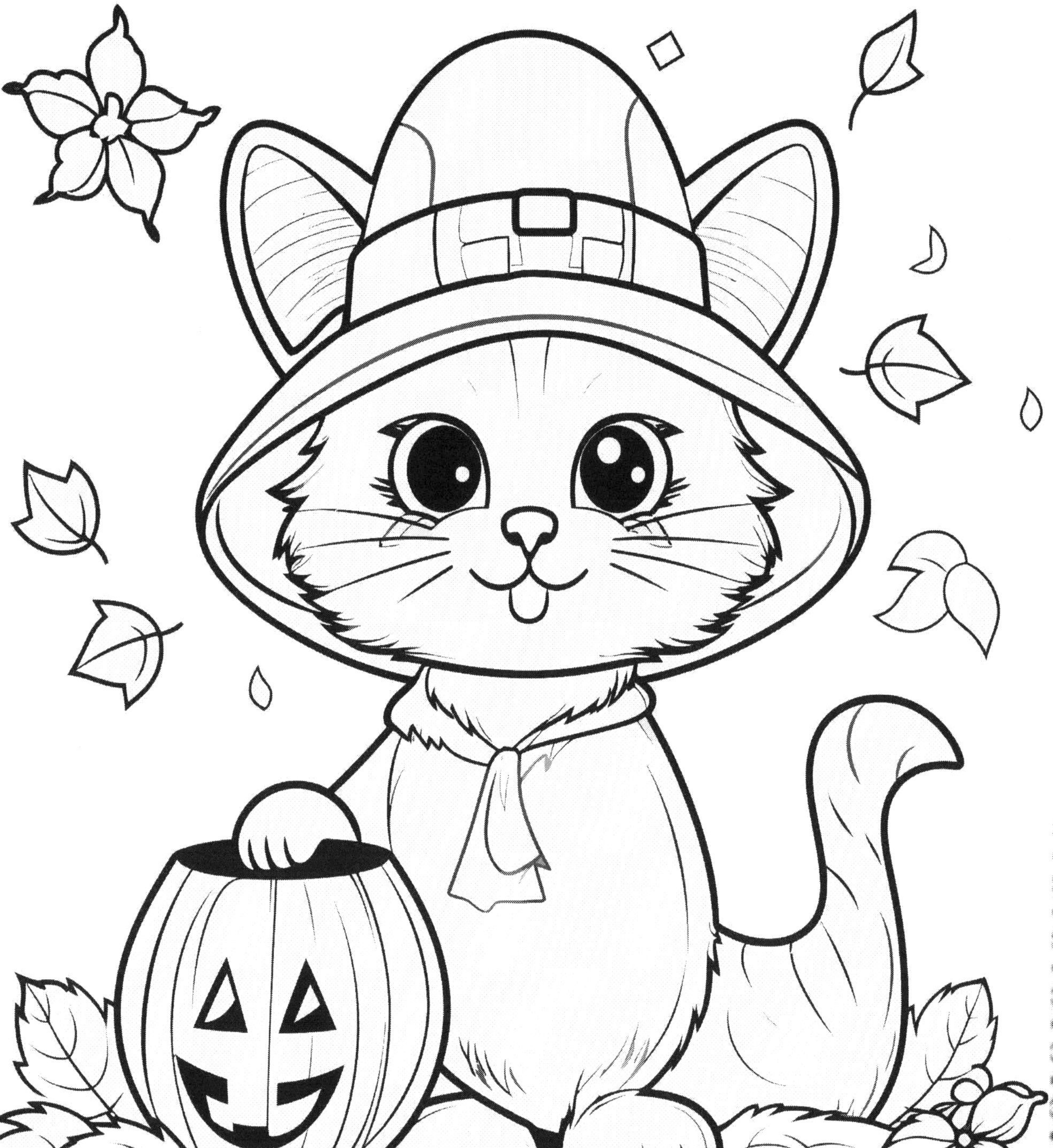

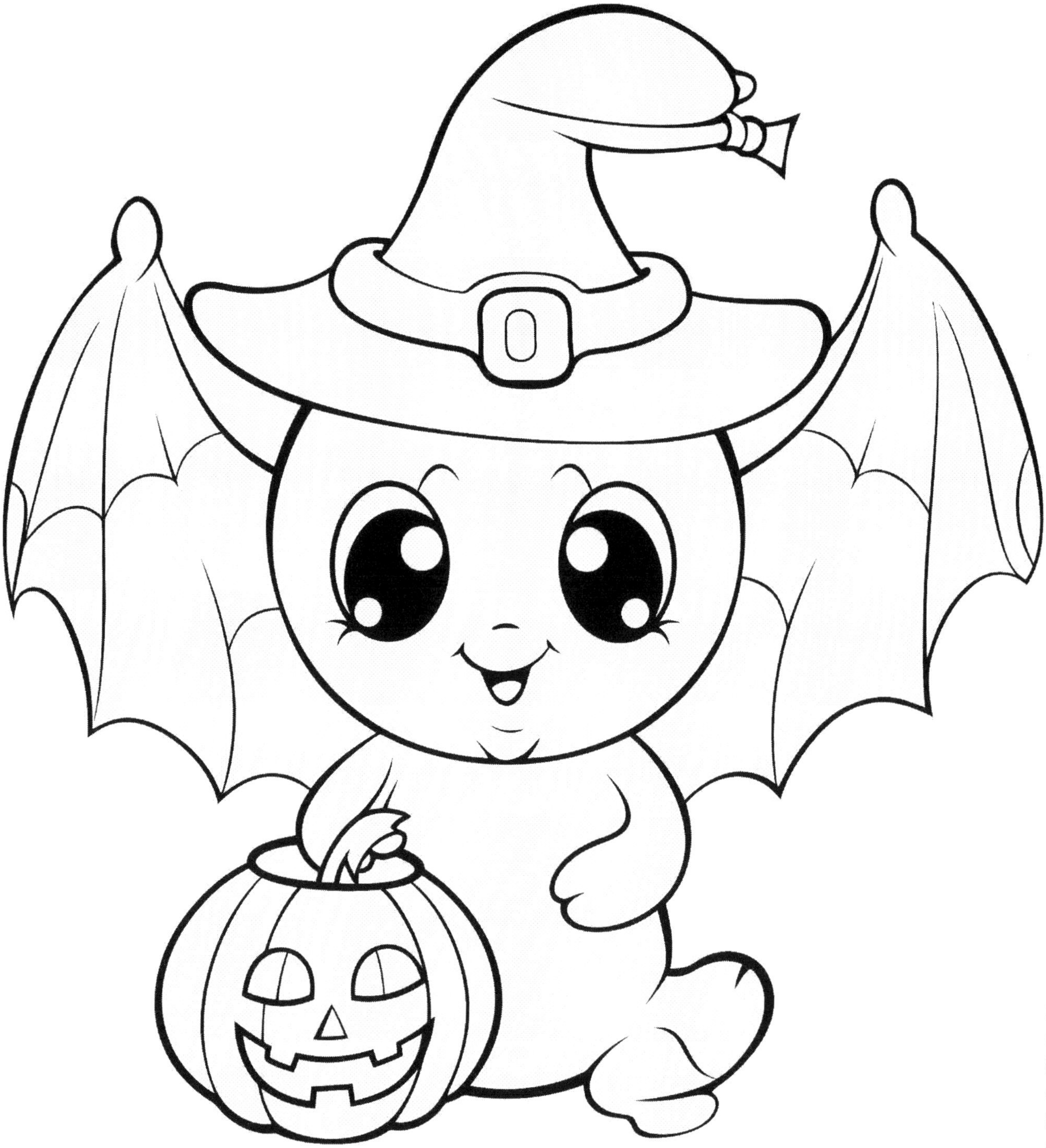

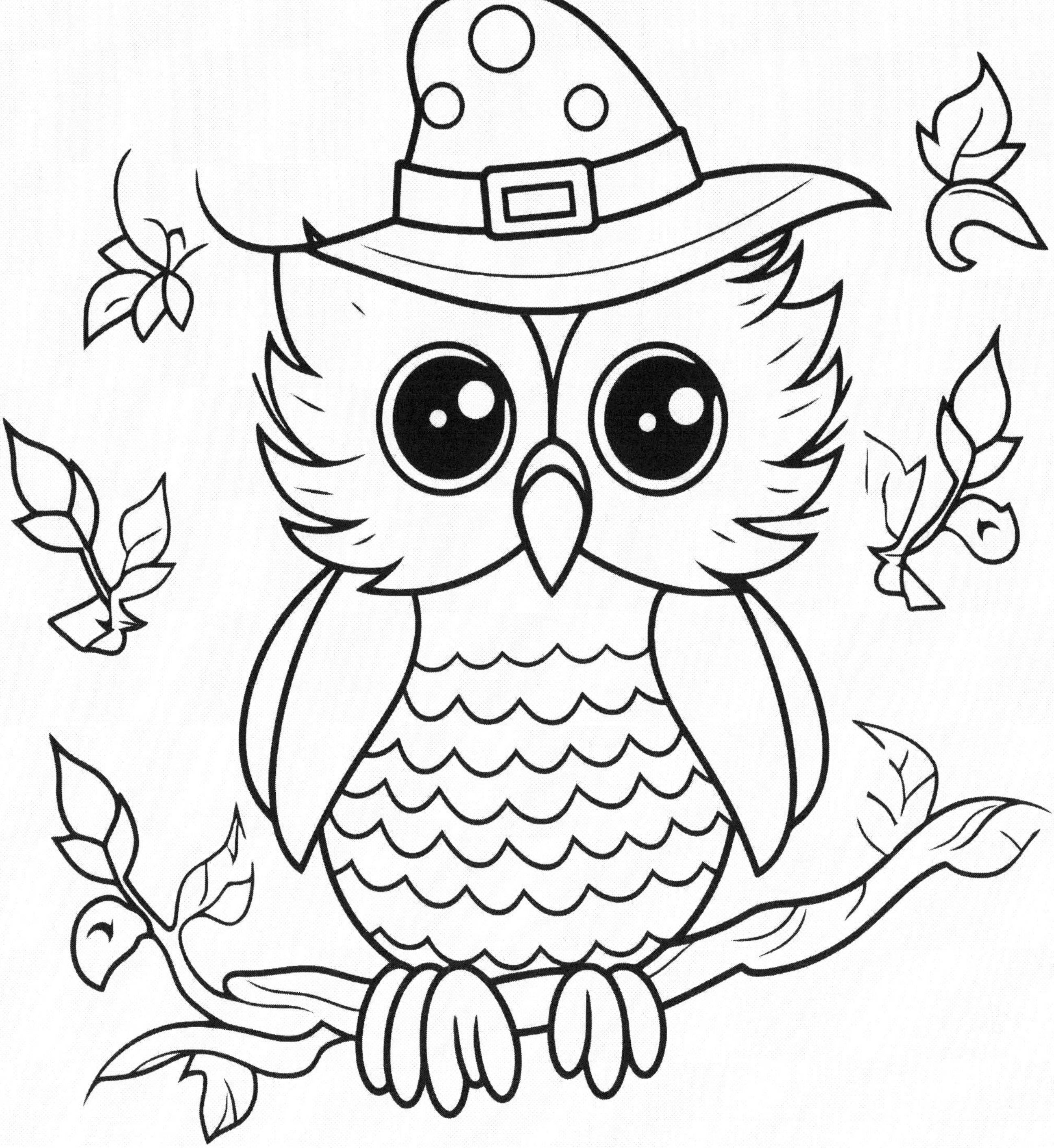

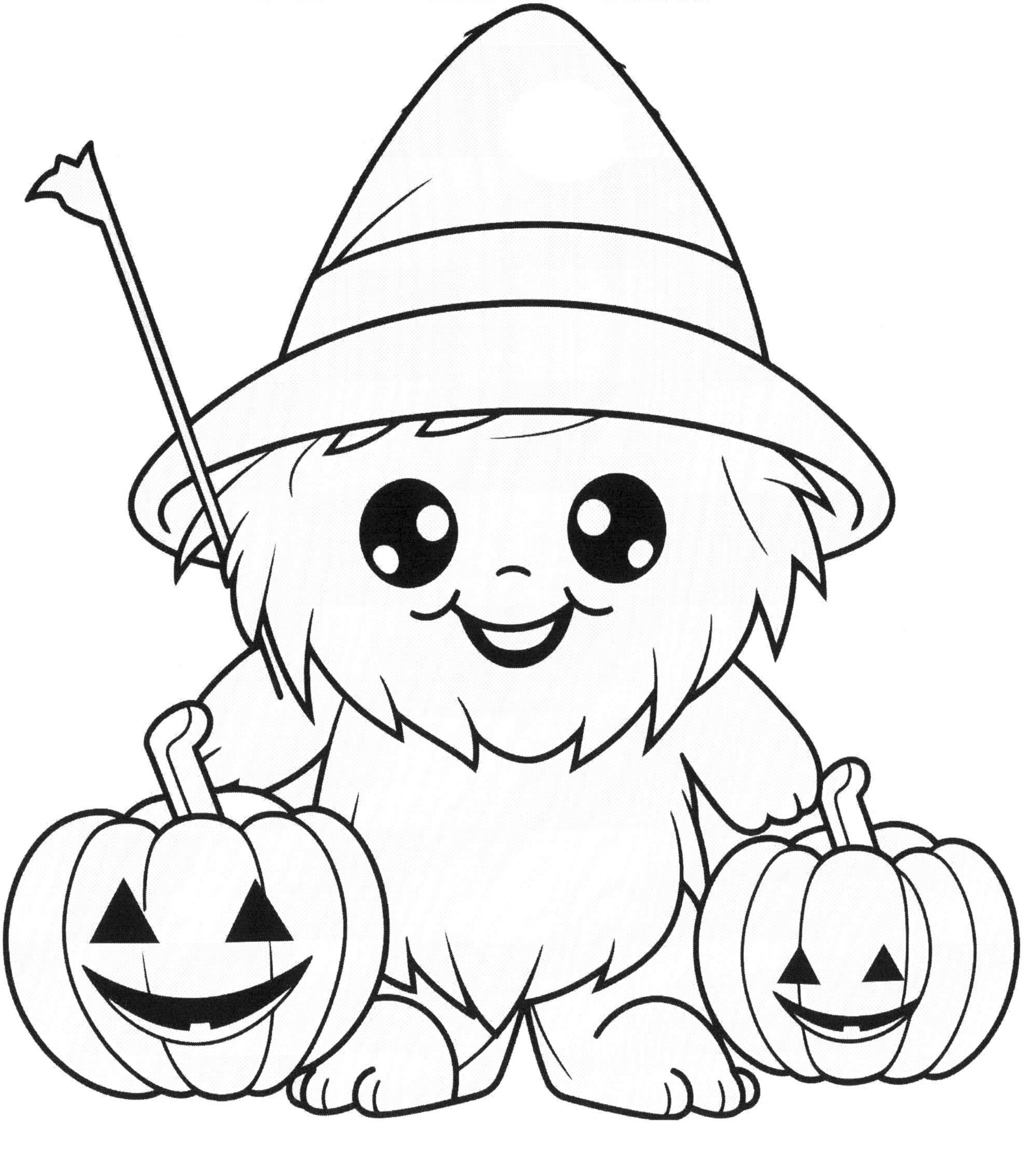

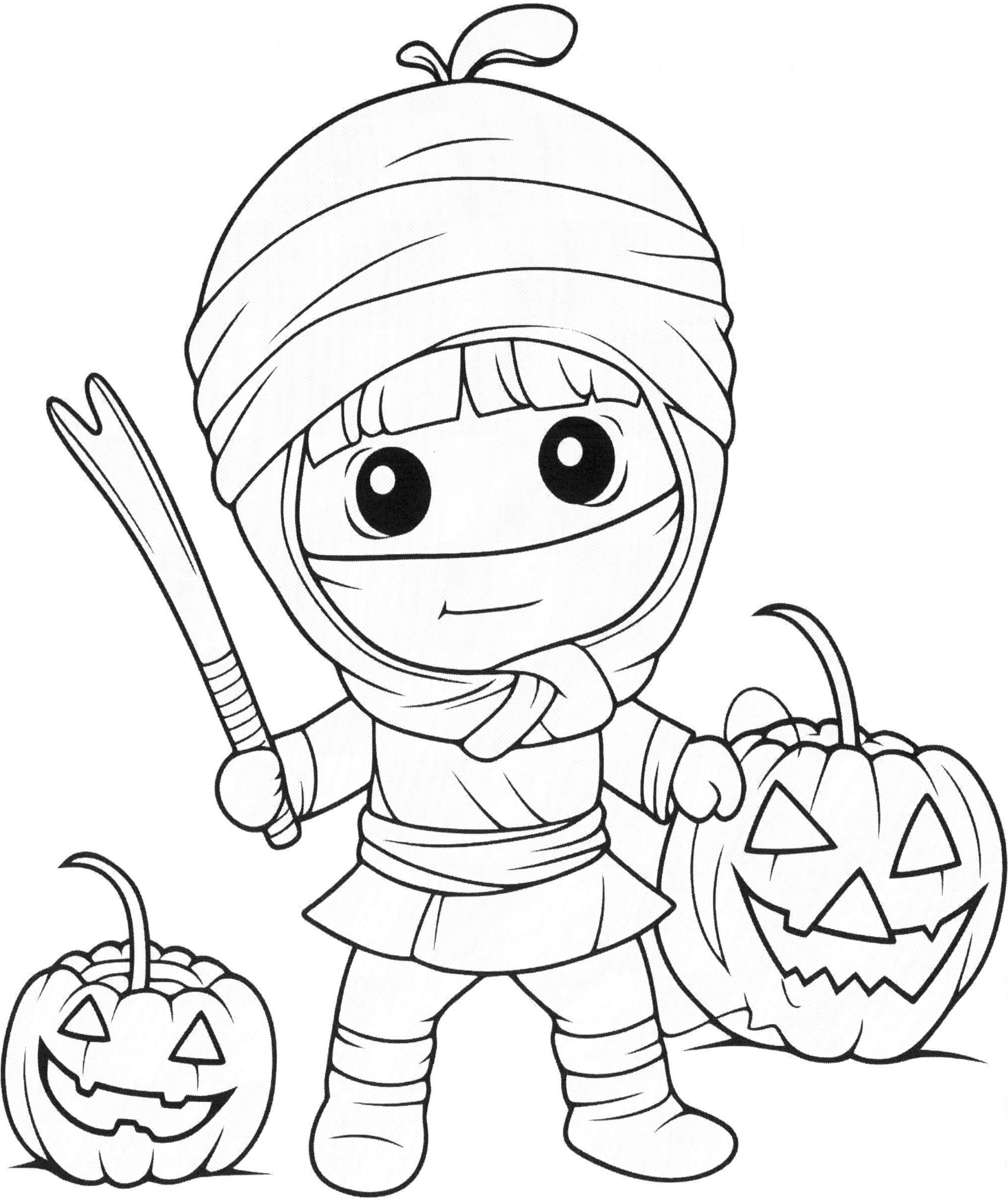

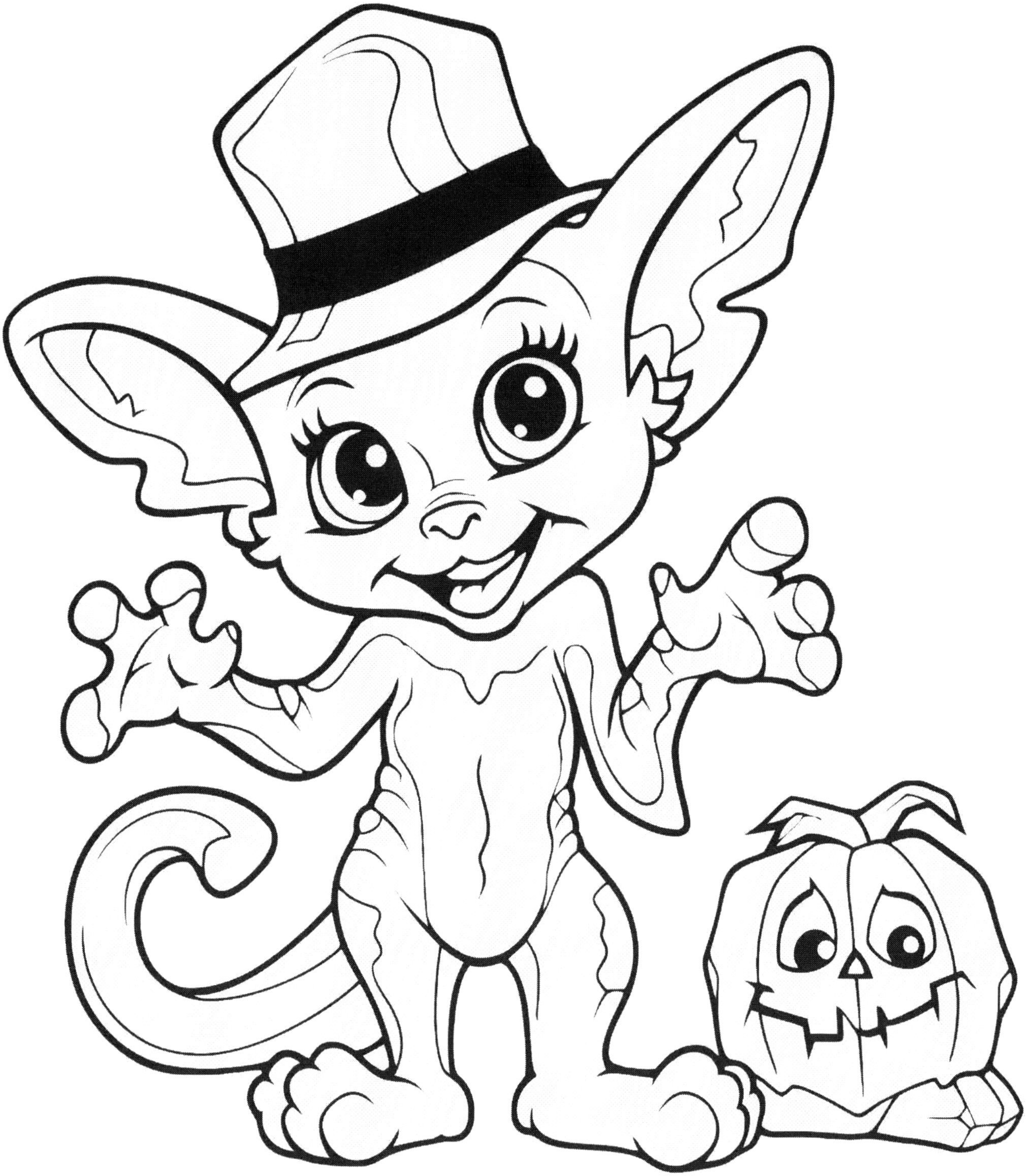

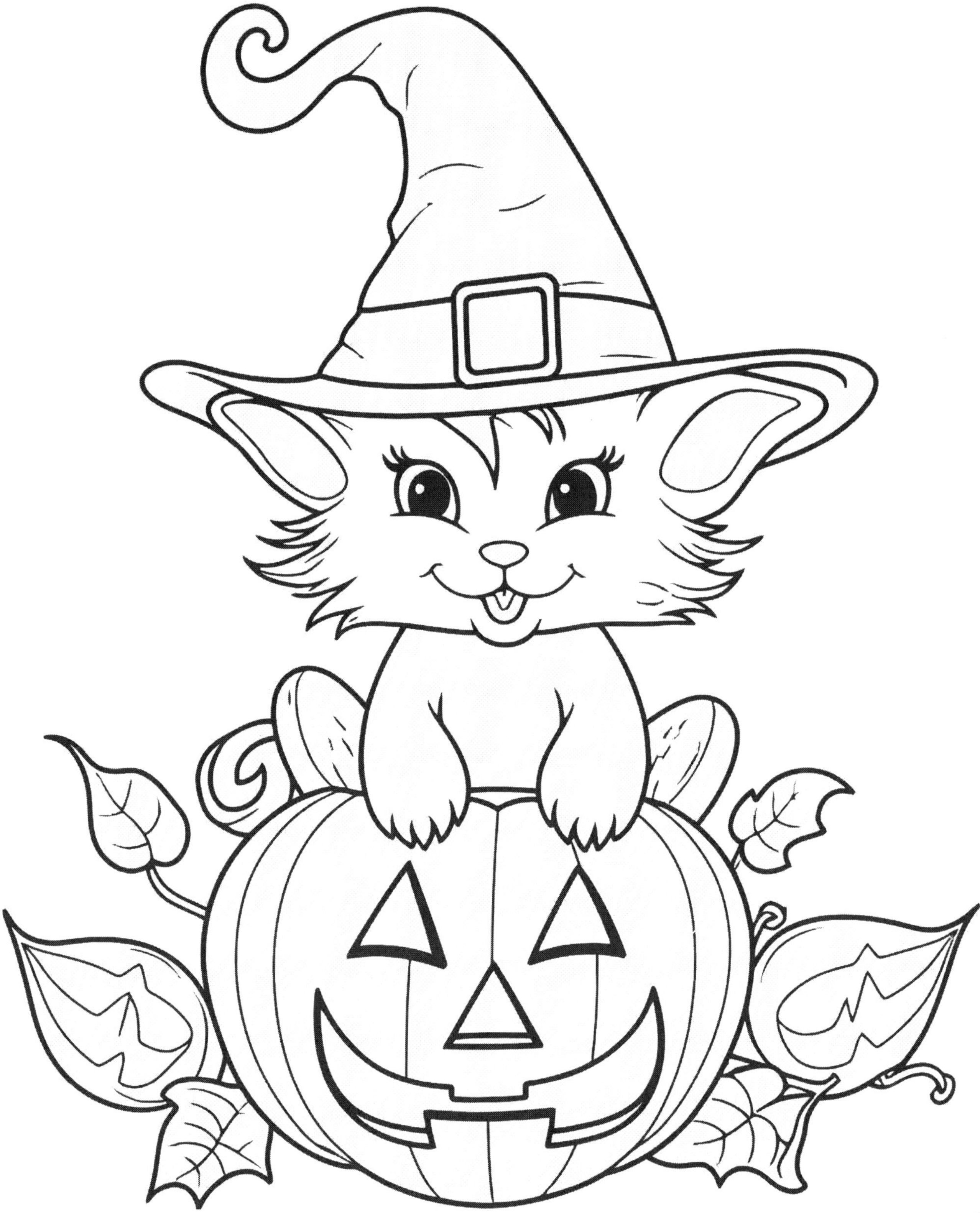

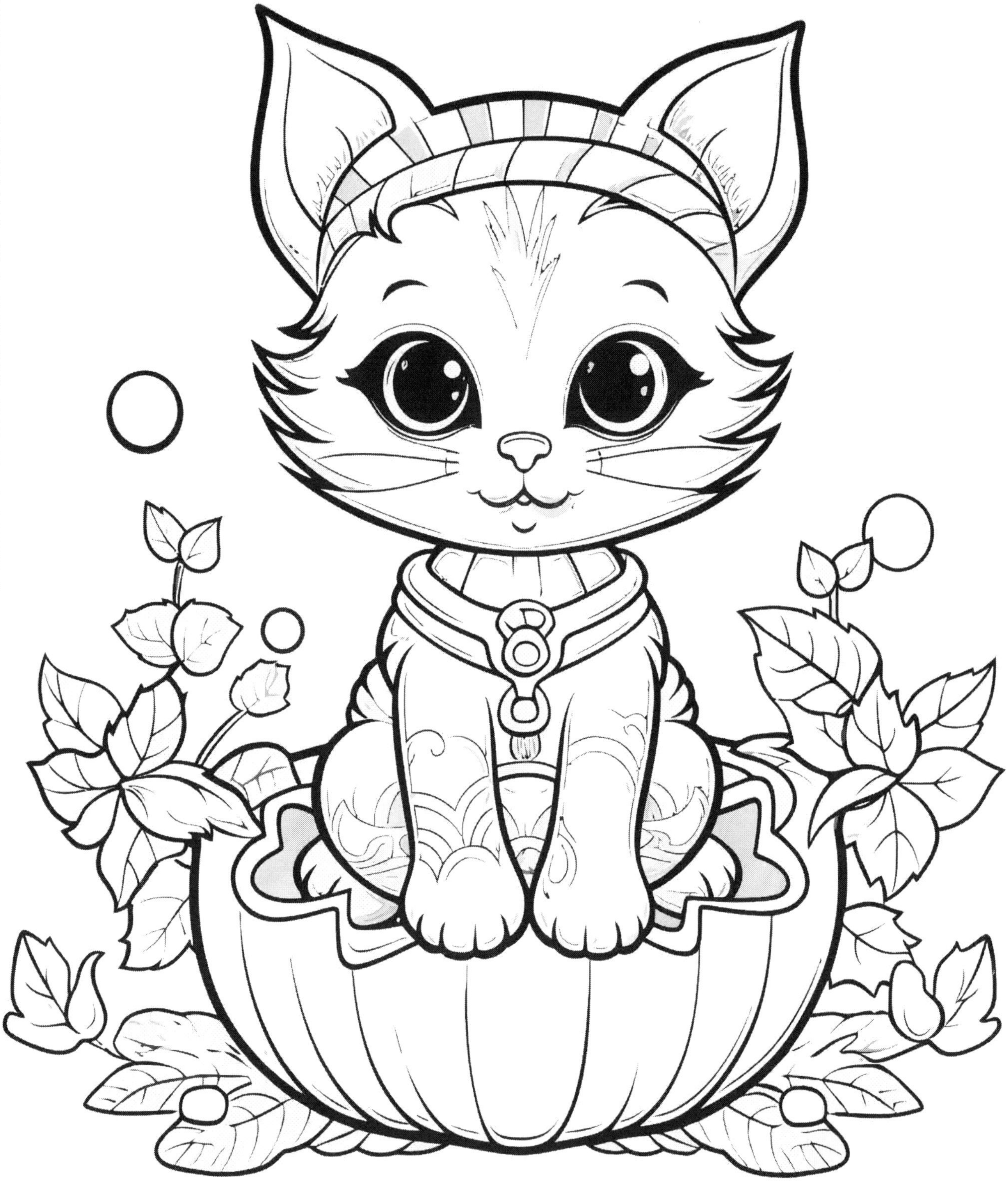

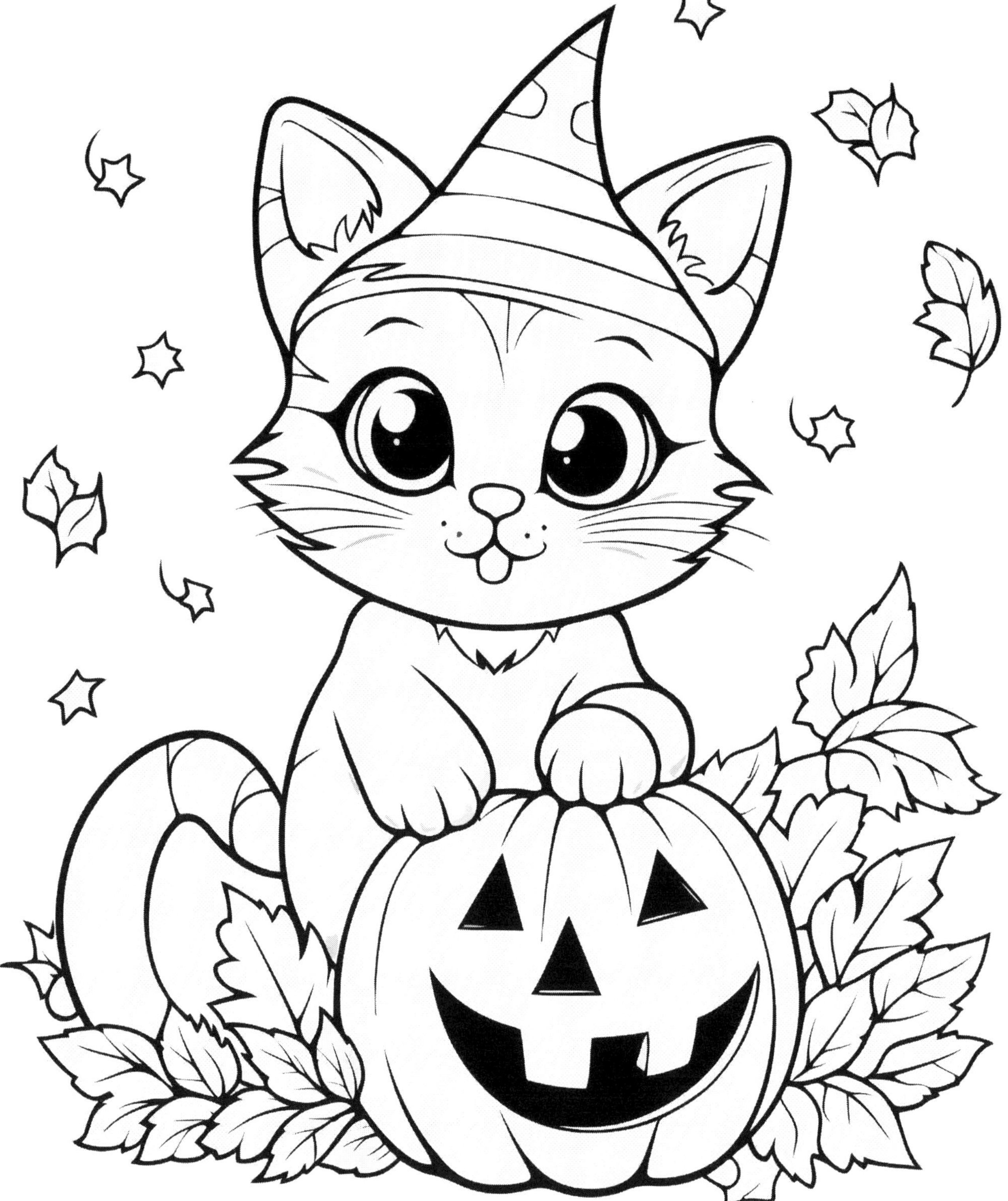

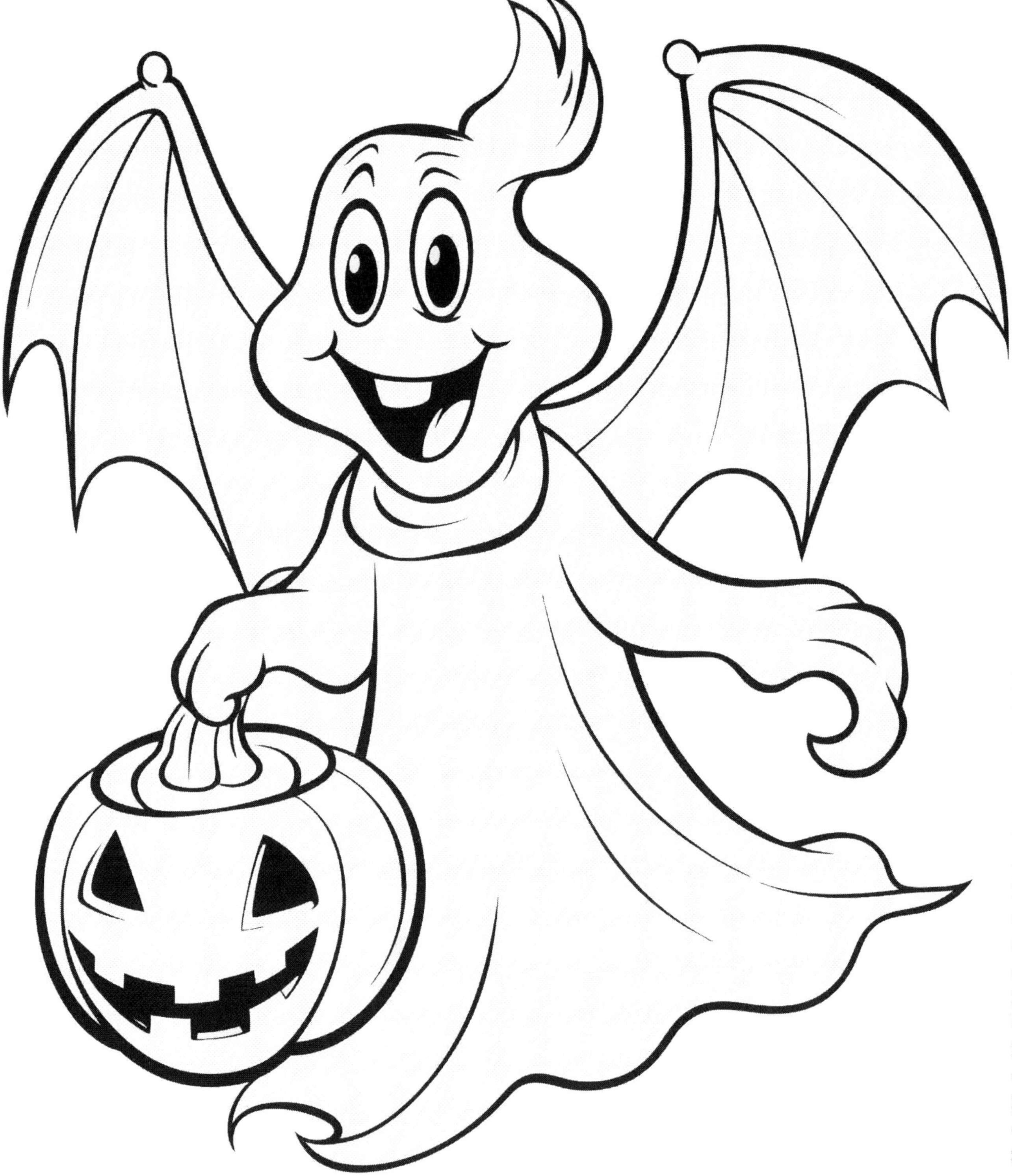

Made in United States
Troutdale, OR
11/26/2023

14991091R00062